His house, His presence. God continues to [...] where He feels at home. Like never before [...] awakening co-laborers who build structures [...] experience more of heaven here and now until He comes.

I have the privilege of calling Michael and Lorisa friends; ever since I met them, their obsession for his presence has infected me. They became specialists in studying what God likes and what He wants to receive, becoming expert hosts of His person. If this is happening in UPPER-ROOM Dallas, I think it is a sign of a small cloud compared to the rain of revival that is coming in the end times, where the focus will not be something but Someone. I desire that intimate people of God would multiply, establishing the first love in the first place, collaborating to transform the earth into a place for His home, His presence.

—**MARCOS BRUNET,**
TOMATULUGAR, Cordoba, Argentina

Jesus is the obsession of the Father's heart and His only sermon. The church is the reward of Calvary, which has been set aside for His one and only worthy Son. Jesus longs to dwell in, with, and in the midst of His possession with a deep passion. This same Jesus has feelings and is a real person. We believe the Lord is looking for churches that prioritize His heart above all else. Houses must emerge that long to move Him, knowing that when His heart is moved, Jesus will gladly touch and change lives. This is the UPPERROOM. This is Michael and Lorisa Miller. They are special and truly called. We have known them and been a part of this move of God since its early days. What God has entrusted them with is sacred and we are deeply blessed by their lives and ministry. When we are with them, we come to receive. I pray you will be as blessed as we have been over these many years of walking together.

—**MICHAEL & JESSICA KOULIANOS,**
Jesus Image

Michael's passion for God and his love for the Body of Christ bleed through the pages of this book. For over thirteen years, I have personally witnessed him pursue the one thing, the face of God, and as a result he has provoked countless others to do the same! I'm honored to call Michael my friend and I know this book will be a catalyst for many pastors and leaders who want to see a greater manifestation of God's presence upon their lives, their families and their spiritual communities.

—PETER LOUIS,
Braveheart Ministries

The deepest longing in the heart of God is to fully dwell on the earth with His people. Just like David, God is raising up leaders and places all over the earth today who will declare that ministry to Jesus and loving Jesus takes precedence over every other ministry and assignment. Michael Miller is one of these leaders, and UPPERROOM is one of these places God is raising up as a witness to the global church that Jesus is not merely a means to destiny but IS the destiny. My family and I were honored to have a front-row seat for over three years in the midst of this community whose sole purpose was hosting and ministering to Him. It changed us forever. I wholeheartedly endorse this author and the message of this book. May God use this book to spark a shift in the church around the world!

—COREY RUSSELL,
Author of *Teach Us To Pray*

Brennan Manning once lamented that many spiritual leaders are like travel agents passing out brochures to places they themselves have never been. This is not the case with Michael and Lorisa Miller.

Since 2004 I've had a ringside seat to their heart and journey. In the early days of our relationship, I was privileged to be their pastor and officiate their wedding. For many years though they, in ways they may not fully realize, have been trustworthy teachers and guides to me in regard to the things discussed within this book.

Two passages of scripture came to mind as I engaged with this book. In Ezra 7:10, Ezra is described as one who committed himself to studying the Word of the Lord, doing the Word of the Lord, and then teaching the Word of the Lord. Note the order. He studied it, did it, and then taught it. When I think about the Millers, this is the order of their lives and ministries. They speak and write from a place of revelation rooted in the Word of God and then informed by their experience of seeking to walk it out. From the earliest days of their union, they've sought to be the kind of people and have the kind of lives upon which the Lord rests. It is out of their experience as a couple, with their own children, and their UPPERROOM family that they speak. From it we can find a wealth of inspiration and practical wisdom and encouragement.

In Matthew 13:52, Jesus spoke of teachers who've been instructed in the kingdom of heaven are like the owner of a house who brings out of his storehouse new treasures as well as old. What Michael and Lorisa "bring out" in this book is a treasure that's been forgotten by many believers and pastors and missed by others, yet it's been there all along in the grand plot line of scripture.

This is my 26th year in the role of a lead pastor and 30th year in full-time ministry. I've read my fair share of books. There's no "complete" book apart from scripture. To use the language of the apostle Paul, "We all know in-part, see-in-part, speak-in-part. How do we convey fully who He truly is and what it means to receive Him in His fullness and live in light of it? The day has yet to come when we will know as fully as we are known. But that day is coming!" Maranatha! In the meantime, I cannot convey how important and needed their "part" – "His House, His Presence" – is in our day and age! It is so needed! I found it to be unflinchingly honest and transparent, insightful, and instructive for the days ahead of us all.

May what Paul told Timothy be true for you as you read this book. "Reflect on what I'm saying, for the Lord will give you insight into all this." (2 Timothy 2:7)

—**CHRIS SEIDMAN,**
The Branch Church Dallas

I truly believe that the book you are holding in your hands contains one of the most relevant messages for our generation. The life of my friend Michael is a message in itself on how to bring the Presence of God into our midst. His life and ministry are a living message on how to build a culture of heaven in the midst of cities. Restoring the centrality of the Presence of God in lives, homes and communities is the priority of the Kingdom for this time. By reading these pages, you will burn again so that His House will once again be the place of His Presence.

—**MARIANO SENNEWALD,**
The Mission Institute, Buenos Aires, Argentina

His House, His Presence

Calling the Church to God's Original Design

Michael Freeland Miller

Edited by Autumn Williams and Lorisa Miller
Cover Design by Neww Creative, Inc.
Cover Art by Hannah Aaron

UPRM

Published by UPPERROOM Global, Inc.
Publisher Website: upperroom.co

Paperback ISBN: 978-1-952421-31-0
eISBN: 978-1-952421-32-7
Library of Congress Control Number: 2023903993

First Edition
Printed in the United States

DEDICATION

This book is dedicated to the community I lead at UPPERROOM Dallas.

There is no greater honor for a leader than to be known first for the people that follow him. I am in awe of the thousands of volunteers that have daily prayed, sung, played instruments and ministered to Jesus throughout the years.

Your collective love for Jesus and His presence has marked the earth.

Thank you for your steadfast and unrelenting YES to loving and ministering to Jesus.

TABLE OF CONTENTS

FOREWORDS

I've been around the block–the church block–all my life, and I can tell you that Michael Freeland Miller's voice is full of wisdom and revelation. In these pages, you will encounter a strong apostolic voice to the church body, especially the American church.

I have run with Michael since early 2008 when I invited him to preach at Lake Highlands Church (LHC), where I was an elder and member over 24 years. I intended to meet him beforehand for a lunch meeting, to "vet" him, but we never left his office after I first arrived. The Lord quickly connected us as a father and son, and a wonderful journey began. After he and Lorisa Littlejohn were married that next month, they were a part of LHC and our Wednesday night small group for almost a year.

The vision to establish a resting place for God's presence in the Oak Lawn area of Dallas began on Passover 2010. That first meeting led to many others until my wife Jane and I felt so called by the Lord to join what God was doing that we sold our suburban home and moved downtown to be near the area and help establish a prayer room. Jane and I had been to IHOP-Kansas City several times and were apprehended by Jesus' prophecy that His house would be called a house of prayer.

Fast forward twelve years - they have been rich, hard, wonderful, and challenging. But you will see in the pages before you that Michael and Lorisa have kept the main thing the main thing, obeying what Jesus said was the first and greatest commandment.

I recommend this book wholeheartedly and without reservation. I was born on Monday night and was in church on Wednesday night. I have been a churchman all my life—and seen it all. And I can tell you that Michael is a trustworthy leader because it is not about him. It is about Jesus. It is about God, who always desires that we create a resting place for Him.

Michael has walked in submission to Godly authority ever since I first met him. I am honored to be a part of the spiritual covering over Michael and Lorisa. It is my life's most important role in the Kingdom and percolating with joy throughout. How truly wonderful and delightful to see brothers and sisters living together in sweet unity. It is as precious as the sacred scented oil flowing from the head of the high priest....Indeed, that is where the Lord has decreed His blessings will be found, the promise of life forevermore.

—Truman Spring
UPPERROOM Dallas, Elder and Staff Pastor

In 2013, I had just completed four years at a Bible Institute. I was so in love with God and hungry for His presence...but I was bored by the church. "Bored" is an understatement–I was disillusioned. My experience for what I had been told church should look like was, for the most part, dull. Something in me knew that there was more to what was being presented every Sunday. I had a deep desire to see God's presence interrupt services. Like a nomad in search of a place to settle, I longed to be somewhere that I knew God's presence rested.

> Did this place even exist? Where was it? Was there something wrong with me?

One of my dear friends from the Bible Institute I attended eventually invited me to a church called "upper room." She claimed I'd really like it, but my immediate thought was cynical because I was essentially done searching for a church that I actually felt at home in. After some convincing, I decided to attend a church service. The best way to describe what I experienced walking into this literal upper room (above a vet clinic), would be comparable to the children in Narnia. Peter, Susan, Edmond, and Lucy entered a world beyond their own as they passed through the wardrobe. In the upper room, I found the One I loved with other people that also loved Him really well. This spoke hope into what seemed to be mundane, "normal" Christianity. The goal of this place was solely Jesus and His presence. I discovered home; I discovered my people; and ten years later, I am still here.

Behind a healthy house, you will always find healthy authority. When those in authority are truly submitted to the authority of God, they will naturally create environments where others can plant their roots deep and bloom. I know this to be true in my life personally through the way

Michael and Lorisa's reckless obedience to the authority of Jesus has affected me, and forever impacted my spiritual growth.

I can vividly remember the first time I met Michael, or really the first time he spoke with me. We had just finished a Sunday night service and people were praying over one another. Unexpectedly, this man who I had not officially met (and had only seen preach from the stage) came up to me and got very close to my face. If you know Michael, you know that he has these intense icy-blue eyes. They reveal the humility of his heart and the deep conviction that he carries. I stood still in my place as he began to give me a prophetic word about rooting myself in this place called "upper room". He said that if I decided to root myself, I would begin to see my life thrive. Michael had no idea who I was or what I was about, but that moment marked me. The fruit of that word is something that I am still living in today. This man has become a big brother and a father to me. His life has been an example of what a man in love with God looks like. I have had the incredible privilege of seeing him gripped with conviction and lead our church to be the Bride Jesus longs for. Time and time again, Michael has kept our house pure. He has taught me when to flip tables and when to honor what only God Himself can do. He has shown me what a committed husband looks like to his bride. He has displayed what a father who pursues his children looks like. He has demonstrated what a leader (who is first a follower of Jesus) looks like. He's taught me about worship more than anyone else I know. Some of my favorite memories of the journey at UPPERROOM have been witnessing Micahel respond to God. I've seen him amidst a crowd of thousands and I've been intimately hosted at his table for a family Shabbat dinner. I can confidently say he has made his entire life a response to God. Michael's life has revealed Jesus to me. I love you, Michael.

Lorisa is someone you only meet once in a lifetime. She carries a deep wisdom, as well as a humble gentleness that cuts through any numb heart. I have seen her throughout the years, in the midst of influence or pain, choose to be tender-hearted towards God. She has deeply marked my life through the way that she has mothered her four beautiful children. I've seen this translate to our entire church body through the way that she preaches–piercing you to your core while also healing you. I have never met another like her. I love you, Lorisa.

Dear reader, I hope that this book marks you with the desire for God to fill every space that you inhabit with His presence. I pray that in every physical building and room in your heart, He would occupy each hall, bedroom, and chamber. After all, we are His temple. We are the house He desires to rest in.

—Joel Figueroa
UPPERROOM Dallas, Worship Leader

INTRODUCTION

God is looking for a resting place.

He who dwells everywhere is looking to dwell somewhere. It is this desire of God, this somewhere He longs for, that is the focus of this book. This somewhere, I believe, is the purpose of God's created order and the end game to all things, including my life and ministry. It is unto this somewhere being established that I live, labor and long for.

From the beginning of scripture to the end, we can see that God desires a dwelling place—a home. This one truth shapes all other realities. This reality shapes all our pursuits. This desire did not originate in our hearts but is found first in His. Ideally, the church–the actual building structures, as well as the ecclesia gatherings of believers everywhere–would be His resting place.

Revivals of new believers and church growth are occurring around the world, especially in closed nations where Christians are being persecuted. However, statistically, we see the Western evangelical church is on a decline and losing the most young, populous and influential generation. I cannot pinpoint how we got here or all the intricacies to the numerous and diverse problems churches face, but the American church as we have known it is on a downward trajectory. Yet, I am not as hopeless as that may sound. Instead, I am keenly aware and anticipating that something drastically must change, and can change, soon.

Secularization of the church is a very real issue many faith leaders are facing today. Across programs and pulpits, we are seeing the gospel be replaced by a man-centered, man-serving, man-focused agenda. At face value, these focuses will seem admirable, even biblical, and Kingdom-centric. But our focus has shifted from being God-centered to self-centered. Some of the largest churches in my city have slogans that we can all agree upon and not question the validity of their purpose.

"We are all about people."

"You belong here."

"Making a lasting difference."

"Loving people and our city."

"A community for all of humanity."

If we pull back the layers of these mission and vision statements, we will discover most churches are built upon either an individual personality or a collective purpose that gives people a sense of community or fulfillment. Look at church growth and the leading influencers in the church over the last few decades: personality, relevance, growth, vision, and strategy are buzzwords that have worked their way to the center of churches and faith leaders' agendas. *Purpose Driven Life* and *Purpose Driven Church* by Rick Warren are two of the most influential books still shaping the life of the modern church and believers today. Their focus is on purpose for the individual or a faith community. A quick survey across the evangelical spectrum will show pastors and personalities who lead with their charisma, gifts, and ability to influence people. How large your congregation and following on social media are now considered the mark of influence and a successful ministry. The more people who are reached, the more effective you are. Leaders pursue and prioritize influence with admirable motivation to see more people reached and impacted.

Again, this seems to be a right and biblical target; after all, Jesus said, "Go into all the world and make disciples." But why isn't this model of influence and propagation of purpose causing real change throughout our world? There is an entire generation of young people deconstructing and leaving the American church. Especially in the last decade, there has been a mass exodus from the Judeo-Christian contexts that the Western church was built upon.

Many leaders believe the solution is to change the message or reinvent the traditional delivery. Social norms have changed so we must change with them—address them in an offensive manner. Addressing the sexual, racial, and political "wokeness" must be the key to influencing people for Jesus today. However, these social agendas are swaying much of the faith community to become more culturally relevant than biblically integrous. Because there are problems, we must proactively respond to the wrong, right? Maybe.

To be the pure and spotless bride Jesus will return for, the church today must be stripped down to the purity of scriptural truth and power of the Holy Spirit to truly reflect the glory of our King and be light and salt to the world around us. Cultural Christianity today is being pruned and church leaders need to welcome this pruning from our good Vinedresser.

I believe that in the coming days "less will be more" for the church of Jesus Christ. I believe we are going to rely, once again, upon the supernatural power of the Holy Spirit to see lives transformed. Beyond our abilities, strategies, giftings, sermons, relevance, reach, services, and programs that we have employed to see growth, we are going to instead grow in conviction that without the presence, power, and leadership of the Holy Spirit, we are useless. Bigger is not better. More is not the goal. Attendance, reach, clicks, and online followers are not a true measure of leadership, influence, or success; Jesus is. We need Him and His leadership.

As a pastor and leader, I am convicted to equip the saints in the sustainable simplicity of following the Lord's leadership, creating a resting place for Him, and ministering first and foremost to Him. This is not a book about my church leadership or you growing in your leadership. These pages before you are about following His leadership. This is not a book I wrote to minister to you or for you to grow in how to minister to others. Undoubtedly, I have discovered the deliverance, rest, sustainability, and joy of leading from this place and prioritization—as a follower first. And I believe you will too.

> AS A PASTOR AND LEADER, I AM CONVICTED TO EQUIP THE SAINTS IN THE SUSTAINABLE SIMPLICITY OF FOLLOWING THE LORD'S LEADERSHIP, CREATING A RESTING PLACE FOR HIM, AND MINISTERING FIRST AND FOREMOST TO HIM.

We will explore the scriptural references that give identity, and therefore application, to the created earth and humankind being the Lord's dwelling place, and the bride of Christ being ministers first and foremost to the Lord. As leaders, it is time to align ourselves with the simplicity and purity of first being a follower of Jesus. Through the life of King David and the expression of worship from Mary of Bethany, we will unpack what the scriptures tell us the Lord desires and delights in. He has preferences described in scripture that we would be wise to heed.

The Lord is pruning, stripping, and shaking everything that can be shaken, and we must embrace His leadership. He is stripping us of the superficiality of cultural Christianity and calling us instead into the depths of His heart. For many of us, this will feel like a burial ground.

I will share how I was personally stripped down to the studs when starting the UPPERROOM. I had to be stripped, shaken, and pruned in order for the Lord to establish the unshakable foundation of Jesus Christ and Him alone. God is in the business of burning up the wood, straw, and hay that we as church leaders have been building with. He is willing and ready to give us the precious jewels, gold, and silver from His everlasting treasury.

This book shares the nuggets of revelation Jesus has given me through the journey of starting the UPPERROOM church and house of prayer in Dallas. I wish to vulnerably share where the Lord has convicted and delivered me into prioritizing His leadership, ministry, and love. For current and future church leaders, I will give examples of how Lorisa and I have practically equipped the corporate body we pastor at UPPERROOM to follow us as we follow Him.

We love Him so much. We love the church, His bride, so much. And we love that we have only just begun. The depth, height, length, and width of the knowledge of Him and His love is endless. Let's dive in together. Like Paul told the Corinthian church, "Our mouth has spoken freely to you...our heart is opened wide" (2 Cor. 6:11). The words, stories, and revelations I offer in the pages that follow are my heart opened wide to you, reader. Like the New Testament church of Acts, may we be of one mind eager to keep the unity of Spirit. Like an epistle to a church, I long to encourage, comfort, and edify you. As members of one body, with Christ Jesus our head, let us link arms, minds, tendons, and hearts in unity under His Lordship and perfect leadership.

Chapter 1

THE UPPERROOM STORY

"God, you called the wrong guy."

It was the fall of 2010. I was six months into being a church planter and I was at the end of my rope. I could not figure out why God had called me to plant a church in the Oak Lawn area near downtown Dallas.

Lorisa and I were still newlyweds when we moved into the Oak Lawn neighborhood, just two blocks from Cedar Springs and Oak Lawn Avenue. If you are not familiar with Dallas, Oak Lawn is the homosexual district, locally coined as the "the gayborhood" of Dallas. From the outside looking in, it was an odd choice for a young Christian couple to make when most of our peers were moving to suburbs, buying homes, and starting families.

Truth be told, we would not have chosen this area of our city to do ministry or plant a church. The reality is that we wouldn't have chosen much about the journey God has led us on. However, we were back then, and are to this day, committed to following His voice and His Spirit no matter what, even when, and especially when, it doesn't make sense.

After a year of marriage, we had entered a season of deep hunger and seeking God for what He wanted to do in and through us. We knew we had a call on our lives, and we wanted Him to lead, at all costs, we just had no clue what those costs would be. We began praying together in our apartment every evening after work, asking for His leadership in our lives, asking for His plans. There were many times we canceled social events just to set aside time to seek Him together in prayer.

It was during this season of pursuit and consecration that the UP-PERROOM was birthed—but it was definitely not because of our strategic planning. It was our death. In fact, we had a plan that we thought would please God, and we were quietly making plans to move to Redding, California. We had kept this decision discreet, knowing that our church community and close friends would be impacted by our move across the country. Moving to California would impact a lot of people, but we were sensing that God had something new for us. We desired to join a church called Bethel, attend their school of ministry, and finish graduate studies at a local college.

These plans weren't just hypothetical. I had landed a pharmaceutical sales job and Lorisa was enrolled to finish her higher education. We had a house picked out to rent and had applied to Bethel's ministry school. Our plans were fairly solidified until "the dinner."

THE DINNER

I call this specific occasion "the dinner" because it would completely redirect our immediate plans and ultimately our life trajectory. It was our first time to have dinner with this couple, but the Lord would use this couple and our short time together to dramatically change the course of our lives.

Upon arriving, I immediately noticed that the wife had brought her Bible and it was open on the table. She smiled as we sat down and after initial pleasantries she said, "I have to share a dream I had about this dinner last night. I'm sure it won't make any sense to you guys, but I must share it out of obedience to the Lord." Lorisa and I were both raised in very conservative church traditions but were beginning to learn that the Lord could speak through dreams, words of knowledge, and prophetic words. Hungry as we were in that season to hear from God, we were "all ears" upon this woman's mention of having a dream about us.

She began sharing, "In the dream, you two showed up to our dinner and I read to you this verse out of the book of Amos." She then pointed to the fifth chapter and the fifth verse of Amos. She read the one line in the verse that she had read in the dream... "Seek Bethel and die. Seek me and live" (Amos 5:5-6). Upon reading the verse, she smiled and said, "I knew you would probably get nothing out of it." Needless to say, we never went to Bethel. In fact, we felt the fear of the Lord so distinctly that we never even mentioned the idea again. It was back to the carpet for us—faces down in prayer, hungry for Him to lead and speak.

PASSOVER

A few months after "the dinner," in early 2010, I was introduced to a business owner in the Oak Lawn area of downtown Dallas. This man owned a chain of veterinarian clinics throughout the Dallas metroplex, and his flagship clinic and corporate offices were in the Oak Lawn neighborhood. Chip, the business owner, and his team had decided to set aside the second floor of this prime business real estate space for Kingdom purposes.

Chip wanted to see how God might use it, and specifically desired for it to be a space that would host worship and prayer. He, along with many others, wanted to see God move in the Oak Lawn area.

In February 2010, with the sound of dogs barking in the background, I walked into what he described as "the upper room" for the first time. The room was about 5000 square feet. It looked like a former corporate office with old cubicles, a low white ceiling, and fluorescent lights. The centerpiece of the room were the southwest windows. From there you had a great view of the iconic skyline of downtown Dallas. Chip knew it was the perfect place to hold times of prayer and worship over our city.

Passover was just two months away. In my personal devotional time with the Lord, He had been speaking to me out of Mark chapter 14 where Jesus instructed His disciples to go into the city and follow a man carrying a pitcher of water. If they followed this servant, they would be led to the servant's master, the owner of a building where Jesus intended to host Passover, the last supper.

When I read Mark 14, I felt like it mirrored what was taking place in my life. I had found the "servant" in my city who introduced me to the owner of a building. This owner (Chip) had made preparations for Jesus and His disciples to gather. At this point, all I knew to do was to be obedient to the Lord and accept Chip's invitation to gather and pray in his upper room.

Passover would be the start date of a prayer meeting that I assumed would last for just a short time until we had greater understanding about next steps. In fact, we targeted our prayer gatherings to meet from Passover to Pentecost. That would be seven weeks in the upper room, allowing us minimal commitment to the neighborhood, but ample time to plan and pray about what God had next for us. I believed in prayer, of course, but I did not want to be on the hook to lead something that I was not fully committed to. Little did I know, God was setting me up big time.

The first gathering was a bit comical, to say the least. I had never hosted a Passover. I'm a Gentile and knew very little about how to legitimately facilitate a Passover Seder. Lorisa and I Googled and printed off the highest-rated Passover instructions we found online and invited a few of our friends. I cannot prove this, but I would put money on the fact that it was probably one of the worst Passover celebrations ever held. Despite our limited knowledge, we pulled it off. People were blessed, and night one in the upper room was deemed a "success" as we gathered at the windows and prayed over the city of Dallas. We sensed the presence of God and that He was pleased with our obedience.

However, we did not really know where to go after the first night. We felt the Lord's pleasure and leadership, and all we knew to do was to open the room every Sunday night to pray weekly until Pentecost. There was little preparation and therefore little agenda. I had a key to the room, an established time to gather, and a hope that God would show up as well.

Over those seven weeks, something beautiful began to unfold that we could not have orchestrated or anticipated. Each Sunday night that we gathered was uniquely marked by God's manifest presence and leadership. The Lord was very intentional and particular with every step we made. He would not let us simply do what we thought we should do. If we wanted to invite friends, He would convict us not to. In fact, we actually asked a handful of friends to not come. We felt that it was important for them to stay in the church community they were in and not attend our Sunday gathering.

Also, it was amazing who would come to these meetings. Divine appointment after divine appointment marked our community each week.

We learned to no longer be surprised when people we did not know would find their way past the dog barking you could hear from the parking lot and up the narrow, unmarked staircase into a large commercial space where we were seeking His face. People who are now some of our dearest friends started coming for no other reason than they met God in that place. Pentecost came and went, and it never crossed our minds to stop gathering. He kept showing up, and we did not want to miss Him.

WRONG GUY

As exciting and organic as that season was, it would be only six months later that I was telling the Lord, "You called the wrong guy." The weekly prayer and worship meeting in Oak Lawn had grown in numbers and people were starting to talk about a possible church plant. When I say growing in numbers, it went from a random twelve people to a consistent thirty-eight who were enjoying the approach we were taking and loving the community and mission to pray for the city. We were doing nothing more than taking communion, worshiping, and praying each week. Yet, in the early days, the presence of Jesus was transforming those attending, including me and Lorisa. As small as it was back then, we both could sense God wanted to do something big.

Even still, I was not certain anything was truly taking root. Church planting is not easy, and church planting in Oak Lawn is virtually impossible. Over the course of a few months, I had seen at least two other church plants come and go in the Oak Lawn area. It was described by one church planter as a "church planting graveyard," and I could easily attest to why he said that.

A few months into the prayer meetings we were hosting, Lo and I decided that we needed to move into the Oak Lawn area. This move was prompted by another move—some of our spiritual parents, Truman and Jane Spring, had told us they were moving from their home of thirty-three years in the suburbs to downtown Dallas to be closer to the Oak Lawn area and be "all in" with what God was doing in our community. They made one request: that we adopt the hours of their home prayer meetings at the upper room. They had been hosting prayer in their home Monday, Tuesday, Thursday, and Saturday from 6:00 to 8:00 a.m. and then again 6:00 to 8:00 p.m. At that time, we were only hosting one solid prayer meeting on Sunday nights. What the Springs were asking of us would extend those prayer meetings from our one Sunday meeting to eight prayer sets during the week. Oh, and their other caveat was that I would attend all the sets. Gulp.

Upon moving into the Oak Lawn area, locally coined "the gayborhood," I got hit on daily. My wife is *really* beautiful, but the dominant demographic in the Oak Lawn area was not interested in her; they were interested in me. I have good friends who are burdened for, and called to minister to, the homosexual community. They are trained, skilled, and understand the complexities of reaching men and women in a homosexual lifestyle. I, on the other hand, did not have the same burden, desire, training, or skill.

Looking back, I had no idea what the Lord was setting me up for. I was a preacher. I had been in ministry full time for almost twelve years and desired to lead a church. Yet, this would not be the type of church I would have chosen to lead. To be honest, I wanted to plant in the suburbs. I knew the suburbs, I "got" the suburbs, I related to those in the "burbs," and I knew how to pastor and reach people there... people like me. The neighborhood of Oak Lawn, on the other hand, was anything but a suburb that I felt competent in.

MY PERSONAL GRAVEYARD

In hindsight, I realize that Oak Lawn was indeed a graveyard—my personal graveyard. The Lord was stripping me of my preferences, my strengths, and my comforts. I found myself cornered by the Lord in every way imaginable during the first year we lived in Oak Lawn. He was addressing my personal aspirations for a life in Christian leadership and rewriting the script of my ideal life and ministry plans.

In the early days, the Lord was so very clear about what we were *not* to do in Oak Lawn. Once we were committed to planting and pastoring a community, I was about to launch into what any trained ministry leader would do—communicate to others our vision, mission, and values. I was going to use a website and social media and marketing to accomplish this. I was going to raise money, draw people and establish a "normal" church.

As with the infamous "dinner," God intervened right on time. Right around the time I bought the web domain uroom.org, a friend of mine called me. She has been a trusted voice in my life who prays regularly for me and my family. On the phone call, she began to tell me what she sensed the Lord telling her about our new community. She said words that would haunt me for the next five years. "I am really sensing the Lord's jealousy for what you are doing in Oak Lawn. The Lord does not want you to mark the community."

After a few questions, trying to get clarification around what she meant by "mark," I understood from her insight that I was not to name, promote, advertise, or tell people about our prayer and worship meetings in Oak Lawn. Right...makes perfect sense for growth. But in obedience, I heeded her warning as a word from the Lord and did not plow ahead with a comprehensive organizational rollout.

Up until that time, we had not even named our gatherings. The name "upper room" was simply the description people called the room we met in—the second-floor office area above the vet clinic. The name UPPERROOM was not something we intentionally called our community; rather it naturally evolved.

Sidenote to any future church planters: I think calling your church Upper Room is a terrible idea. The inherent historical pressures of being an Upper Room are crazy—especially when Pentecost rolls around each year. Everyone expects something significant to happen with a name like that!

The testimony of the Lord was to be the "mark" of all that we were doing. He said that He would mark it, He would draw whom He wanted, He would give us vision when it was time. We were to depend on Him to move and touch people's lives. I was to trust that His presence would come every time we gathered and that as people encountered Him, they would be like the Samaritan woman and tell others about where to find Him. So much for a website, social media profiles, podcasts, or any other platforms I had wanted to employ to reach people, grow a crowd, and feel a better sense of control in monitoring and evaluating growth or success.

GROWTH

Well, to our surprise, growth came! As the community grew the questions grew as well. Where are we going and what are we doing? My answer continually was one and the same: We are called to pray regularly and wait for direction. We are not gathering for anyone other than the Lord. He is our goal. He is our desire. He is our pursuit.

Over and over, I would share this with people. But if I am honest, as the leader, I felt very insecure. I felt like I was disappointing or confusing people with my answers. I felt like I came across as an incompetent pastor and leader. The questions were sincere and very relevant. Do we have plans for a children's ministry? Do we plan on taking offerings? Are we a church? Are we going to open ways for the community to gather beyond our prayer meeting? All the questions were valid. I wanted answers to these questions as well, and with my training and experience, I was certainly capable of answering them. This was not only in my ministry training, but in my DNA to organize and structure a community, yet the Lord was not letting me put any "traditional" plans together.

Early on, we decided that we had to offer something to families with little children. Our services were lasting sometimes three hours and parents were really being stretched, especially on a Sunday night. At the time, Lo and I did not have kids so I could not fully empathize with what they were experiencing. Now, as a father of four (all under ten years of age), I can't imagine how difficult our meetings were for them. At one point, I assigned my wife to oversee our children's ministry. It was not from God, but I was so tired of disappointing parents by not offering anything to kids that I volunteered Lorisa to fulfill that role.

It was not my best move—as a pastor and especially as a husband. The truth was that God was not calling us in that season to oversee kids. But I thought we needed to address these demands because it was an obvious need, and a relevant challenge all the young families attending expressed to us. How hard could it be to oversee a dozen kids under the age of ten? The answer was impossible. It was impossible because God was not asking us to start a children's ministry then. He was focused on us first learning to follow Him—His voice, leadership, and instructions.

Eventually, He brought the person He had anointed to work with children, and at the time He appointed. It was all about following and waiting on Him.

JANE

The actual weekly prayer meetings would prove to be another death for me. Most of the time, no one came to the prayer gatherings (especially the ones that started at 6:00 a.m.). I wasn't even upset since I am not a morning person myself. I did not enjoy waking up to host a meeting where sometimes I was the only one attending. Prayer was boring—it felt unproductive, and therefore utterly unenjoyable to me in the early days.

Jane Spring was, and still is, a spiritual momma in my life. For years, Lorisa and I had prayed for spiritual mothers and fathers, both for us personally, but also for the young people we were leading. We needed older, wiser, and seasoned saints who had a hunger for the presence of God and move of the Holy Spirit. God answered our prayers by giving us Jane and Truman Spring.

As much as I loved her, I did not really understand Jane's passion for prayer. For several years she had hosted weekly prayer meetings in her home. They were meant to be for the local church community where they attended at the time. It was her way of establishing a house of prayer alongside their church. Yet, people from her church only rarely came to her prayer meetings. Before we had started meeting in Oak Lawn, when I was just becoming friends with the Springs, I attended one of their prayer meetings and her husband and I were the only ones there.

Since that time, the relationship forged with Truman and Jane, both in and out of the prayer room, has been one of the greatest gifts in my life. It has changed our lives, strengthened our marriage, and kept us on the course the Lord had for us to run. Acts 2 says that when the Holy Spirit is poured out, old men will dream dreams and young men will see visions. I had always interpreted this to mean that older men will have dreams in the night from God, and young men will have visions from the Holy Spirit. While this is a correct way to interpret that scripture, I see how that prophecy has played out in our lives and relationship.

The vision of the UPPERROOM was actually a dream of a spiritual mom and dad. When I adopted the prayer hours of Jane and Truman's prayer house at the UPPERROOM, I was finding the vision that God had for my life. As the story unfolded, I realized that dying to myself as I submitted to Jane and Truman's dream for a praying community, became the fertile soil that birthed the vision and DNA of all I am leading at UP-PERROOM today. Their dream became my vision.

Truth be told, prayer in the early days of UPPERROOM was a bore. We had no live musicians and only one, sometimes two worship leaders. Most of the musicians and worship leaders from our Sunday gathering could not make a weekday prayer meeting, so we just played worship music from an iPod on a small speaker and sat in the corner by the windows overlooking downtown Dallas for two hours. In those early days, Jane would pray the same thing at almost every prayer meeting. She would ask the Lord for musicians, and she would ask the Lord for marriages and babies. She wanted young people who could sing, play music, fall in love with each other, and have families. In 2013 (three years after Jane first started praying this), I officiated twenty weddings from our UPPER-ROOM community. The prayers of Jane availeth much.

SWEET CORRECTION

Eventually those early prayer meetings became the center of what we planted our entire community and family around. We did not focus on programs, evangelism, and traditional ministries. We focused on prayer. We did not have a newcomer's interest class—we just told anyone new who wanted to get involved to commit to a weekly prayer meeting.

Over time, the Lord delivered me of boredom in the place of prayer. I realized that it was the primary and most rich way to connect with the Father, the presence of Jesus, and the ministry of the Holy Spirit. I grew in passion and conviction not just about what we were doing in our prayer meetings, but how we were doing it. I grew in the revelation of the first commandment—to love and minister to Him first—and how to fulfill it in our small prayer meeting settings. God met me in that corner at 6:00 a.m., in the most unlikely of places, to teach me how to personally love Him and lead others to do the same in a regular corporate expression.

Remember my exasperated prayer to the Lord about finding the wrong guy? It became a daily prayer of surrender for over a year. I was the wrong guy on all fronts, but in my discomfort and defeat, I became desperate for Him to lead and live in me. He can do anything with a living sacrifice.

After a year of defeated and exasperated prayers, He shattered every paradigm that I had of ministry in one conversation. This conversation would bring me such correction and direction regarding what He was calling me to do. It was the middle of another day, complaining to the Lord that I did not want to run daily prayer meetings in the homosexual neighborhood of Dallas, and the Lord interrupted my sob story with, "Michael, I did not call you to Oak Lawn to minister to people. I called you to Oak Lawn to minister to me." It was from that moment my perspective on prayer and ministry completely changed and I knew my calling was birthed. His voice has a way of doing just that.

The phrase "minister to me" challenged every paradigm of ministry I had. It would reprioritize my vision, goals, and focus. This kind correction from Him would forever change me and the people that I lead. It has become one of the sweetest and most life changing words I have ever received from Jesus, and it has strengthened and sustained me and Lorisa in the past twelve years of ministry.

The early days of the UPPERROOM were unto the Lord stripping me bare. His ways are not our ways. His ways are better and more effective. He was so jealous for this story—this ministry to Him—that He literally stripped me of all that I knew and desired to reveal something so precious: that His leadership is sufficient and so much better than mine.

As I have submitted and sat under the Lord's leadership, He has taught me the things I now offer to you in the pages that follow. What the Lord has personally convicted me of are from His Word, from His Spirit's counsel, and from hours of sitting in His presence, asking for the leadership of the Spirit and Word to direct my days and decisions.

My conviction has grown beyond my personal life and even my local church leadership. He is pruning what is no longer needed and bringing His bride back to a pure and simple devotion to Him. He is stripping leaders of our strategies and formulas that sadly have caused His bride to be busy, distracted, and tired. We are called to be radiant, at rest, overflowing. He desires a resting place upon His people, and when His presence comes to dwell in and upon us, He will give us rest.

Chapter 2

GOD'S TEMPLE-CITY

The Bible is an unfinished story. The whole of scripture is consistent yet unconcluded. From Genesis to Revelation, a story of redemption is still unfolding.

The final two chapters of the Bible are the restoration of the first two chapters of Genesis. From Eden's creation to the earth's re-creation in Revelation, we see the plan of redemption being fulfilled. The crux of His plan, as seen in these two bookends of His Word, is God's desire to dwell with man.

The objective of God's mission is to reconcile and redeem all of humanity and all of creation to Himself. From the original creation of heaven and earth to the future establishment of a new heaven and a new earth, a consistent story has, and is, unfolding. At its core, the God of the universe is restoring the broken relationship between Creator and His creation.

> THE WHOLE OF SCRIPTURE IS CONSISTENT YET UNCONCLUDED. FROM GENESIS TO REVELATION, A STORY OF REDEMPTION IS STILL UNFOLDING.

The fundamental truth, and the climax, is God's Son, Jesus Christ.

Jesus became a man, lived a perfect life, died a sacrificial death, was supernaturally resurrected, and gloriously ascended back to His Father. But the story did not end there. Ultimately, He will return as the universal reigning King.

It is imperative that we understand the finished-yet-still-unfolding tension of the day we live in. The overarching thesis of scripture is about Jesus Christ—and while the work of salvation has been accomplished, His eternal plan of redemption is not yet finished.

Peter's gospel in Acts 3:19-21 (NASB) depicts the past, present, and future realities of the gospel.

> Therefore, repent and return, so that your sins may be wiped away, in order that times of refreshing may come from the presence of the Lord; and that He may send Jesus, the Christ appointed for you, whom heaven must receive until the period of restoration of all things, about which God spoke by the mouths of His holy prophets from ancient times.

The results of Peter's message were clear. If you repent and return, three things will result: 1) your sins will be forgiven (past); 2) times of refreshing may come from the presence of the Lord (present); and last, but not least, 3) Jesus will come back to restore all things (future).

The glorious return of Jesus will bring the final and full redemption of all things. At that moment, every promise, covenant, and prophecy in scripture will be fulfilled. You and I are closer than ever before, even at the reading of these very words, to seeing it fulfilled. Understanding the end game of scripture, the eternal intention of God, is the only way to healthily navigate the seasons ahead.

As leaders, we must keep the end in sight and lead in the present from the perspective of what lies ahead of us. Let me be clear: God is coming back to restore a resting place for Himself on the earth. This was His plan from the beginning. God desires a sanctuary on earth for Himself.[1] Since the formation of Eden, He has designed humankind to dwell, in His likeness, with Him in that sanctuary. This is His chief desire, and because we are His creation, it is our ultimate destiny. The primary purpose of creation was, is, and will be, a home for Him. It was made by Him, through Him, and for Him.

GOD'S ORIGINAL HOME

When we begin to see Eden as a sanctuary, we understand God's purpose in creating it. The design of Eden was accomplished in the first six days of creation. He, with great intent and precision, designed this Eden as a temple-city for Himself.

As the psalmist greatly expresses in Psalm 19:1-2, "The heavens are telling the glory of God; and the firmament proclaims his handiwork. Day to day pours forth speech, and night to night declares knowledge." Creation is unto the knowledge of the Creator. God's desire for a sanctuary in Eden was God's desire to be known, encountered,

> THIS IS HIS CHIEF DESIRE, AND BECAUSE WE ARE HIS CREATION, IT IS OUR ULTIMATE DESTINY.

enjoyed, and worshiped; it is the primary purpose of a sanctuary.

The garden of Eden, the first sanctuary, was the dwelling place for God and humankind to be together. The Genesis 1 and 2 sanctuary concept in

---

[1] Beale, Gregory K. *Eden, The Temple, and the Church's Mission in the New Creation.* Journal of the Evangelical Theological Society, March 1, 2005, pg.7

17

the creation story is often overshadowed by the modern-day argument of creationism versus evolution. Yet, the Ancient Near East understanding of the opening chapters of Genesis anticipate the creation of an extraordinary temple-city where God will dwell in harmony with humanity.[2]

The seventh day is evidence of this design. The day of rest is the climax of the creation account. The first six days led to the seventh day. God rested on day seven. He could have done anything on that day. In fact, there did not necessarily need to be a day seven. After all, God was not tired, He did not need to rest in the manner we think of rest. The work of creation was not tiring for Him—He simply spoke we are and now see. We also know that God did not rest from His work because there was more to do. He rested from His work because it was completed. He rested because creation was finished.

J.H. Walton puts it this way:

> On the seventh day we finally discover that God has been working to achieve rest. This seventh day is not a theological appendix to the creation account, just to bring closure now that the main event of creating people has been reported. Rather, it intimates the purpose of creation and the cosmos. God does not set up the cosmos so that only people will have a place. He also set up the cosmos to serve as his temple in which he will find rest in the order and equilibrium that he has established.[3]

Again, this rest is not due to exhaustion; it was the conclusion of creation and signified completion. This was the desired goal of the created

---

[2] Alexander, D. T. *From Paradise to the Promised Land: An Introduction to the Pentateuch* (3rd ed.). Baker Academic. 2012. Pg. 119

[3] Walton, J. H. *Creation in Genesis 1:1–2:3 and the Ancient Near East.* Calvin Theological Journal, 48–63. 2008.

order—to supply a resting place for the Creator Himself. God, the cosmic builder, rested in and upon what He had created. J.R. Middleton writes:

> Suppose we press the question, what sort of building is God making in Genesis 1? Although not immediately obvious, the unequivocal answer given from the perspective of the rest of the Old Testament is this: God is building a temple. The notion of the cosmos as a temple has its roots in the ancient Near Eastern world view, in which temples were commonly understood as the royal palaces of the gods, in which they dwelled and from which they reigned.[4]

This temple-city theme is continued forward into Eden. The original purpose of the garden was not agricultural nor merely occupational for man, but communal for God and man to dwell together.

Rest was not necessary. Yet, this rest was God revealing to us why He created earth and the cosmos: it was to be His home. A significant dynamic in Eden was God's manifest presence. After all, a home is more than brick, mortar, design, or container. A home is unto someone living inside the created structure.

The activity of God in Genesis 3:8 reveals God coming to His home. In Eden, God was described as "walking in the garden in the cool of the day" (Gen. 3:8). The word for walking in Hebrew is *hithallek*, meaning "to walk back and forth." This walking back and forth by God in the garden reveals a coming and going. He who dwells everywhere at all times came and went.

The omnipresent God made Himself especially present. He would manifest Himself by walking in and out of the garden. This presentation

---

[4] Alexander, *From Paradise to the Promised Land: An Introduction to the Pentateuch,* 123.

of Himself was for intimacy and connection with Adam and Eve. When we accept Eden as the first sanctuary, we understand then that Adam was the first priest. They communed together, they enjoyed creation together, they reigned on earth together.

God manifested His being in a time (coolness of the day) and a space (Eden) to be with man. The design of Eden was to fulfill God's desire for a temple-city for humankind and God to dwell together. But in Genesis 3:9, as His presence came into the garden, Adam and Eve were hiding. Some of the most gut-wrenching words were when God asked a simple, yet profound question of man, "where are you?"

We see the word *hithallek* is used to describe God's presence in later sanctuaries. For example, Moses was given a detailed design for the tabernacle, where God said, "I will also walk (*hithallek*) among you and be your God, and you shall be My people" (Lev. 26:12).

THE DESIGN OF EDEN WAS TO FULFILL GOD'S DESIRE FOR A TEMPLE-CITY FOR HUMANKIND AND GOD TO DWELL TOGETHER.

The same concept of work and rest is depicted in the Mosaic covenant. On Sinai, blueprints for a sanctuary are given to Moses to build a sanctuary. In Exodus 40:32-33, after weeks, if not months, of instructing leaders in the building of God's prescribed sanctuary, Moses "finished the work." And after finishing the work, the Lord responds. Exodus 40:34 states "The cloud covered the tent of meeting, and the glory of the Lord filled the tabernacle." This cloud and glory are the coming (*hithallek*) of God into His sanctuary. Immediately upon the completion of the sanctuary God designed, we see the omnipresent God coming in a specific time and space to manifest His presence in a place prepared for Him.

Again, in Deuteronomy 23:14, God promises to "travel (*hithallek*) along with your camp, to save you and to hand over your enemies to you." These patterns of coming and going mirror the Edenic nature of God's relationship with Adam—God communing with man in time and space.

GOD AND ADAM

The pinnacle of God's creation was man and woman created in His image. The sixth day of creation was the day of mankind—which God declared "very good." Upon His finished work of creation, He began His rest. It is on this first day of rest we see Adam's first day of life. The first twenty-four hours that Adam walked, breathed, and moved on earth was in God's finished work and rest. Adam was created to live in God's rest.

We know Adam was given duties in the garden. These duties were to steward and tend to what God had created. Adam was the steward of the temple-city (creation) that God was resting in. The co-labor aspect was about expanding the God-city of Eden to cover the earth: "Be fruitful and multiply, and fill the earth, and subdue it; and rule over the fish of the sea and over the birds of the sky and over every living thing that moves on the earth" (Gen. 1:28).

These duties were about stewarding and tending to what had already been created by God, stewarding all He had deemed "good."

ADAM WAS CREATED TO LIVE IN GOD'S REST.

In fact, if you study the verbs used to describe Adam's duties in the garden, the description undeniably foreshadows the priestly duties in the tabernacle and Jerusalem temple.

G.J. Wenham comments on this:

> The garden of Eden is not viewed by the author of Genesis simply as a piece of Mesopotamian farmland, but as an archetypal sanctuary, that is, a place where God dwells and where man should worship him. Many of the features of the garden may also be found in later sanctuaries, particularly the tabernacle or Jerusalem Temple. These parallels suggest that the garden itself is understood as a sort of sanctuary.[5]

The parallels outlined here by G.J. Wenham, between Eden and later sanctuaries, are evident by the duties prescribed to both Adam and later Levitical priests.[6]

1. The Lord would walk in Eden as He would the tabernacle (Gen. 3:8).
2. The East Gate is the entry for both Eden and tabernacles (Gen. 3:24; Exod. 25:18–22; 26:31; 1 Kings 6:23–29).
3. The Menorah symbolizes the tree of life (Gen. 2:9; 3:22; cf. Exod. 25:31–35).
4. The river flowing through Eden resembles the river (Ezekiel 47).
5. Gold and onyx are mentioned in Genesis 2:11-12 and are used as decor in the later temples (Exod. 25:7, 11, 17, 31).

The Hebrew verb "*abad*" is used to describe Adam's assignment in the garden and has fascinating parallels to the priestly duties. The word encapsulates two Hebrew verbs meaning to work, to serve, to title, to

---

[5] Wenham, G.H., *Sanctuary Symbolism in the Garden of Eden Story*, PWCJS9 (1986): 19.
[6] These parallels are set out by Wenham in ibid., 19-25.

keep, to observe, or to guard. These verbs, when used in isolation, can be attributed to several activities. Yet, when arranged the way they are arranged in Genesis 2, in God's instructions to Adam, the words directly relate to the duties of the priests in later books. They parallel one another, which again leads us to conclude that Adam was a priest in the sanctuary of Eden. Man was first appointed to protect and guard the sacred space of Eden, not simply to garden it.

God's temple-city construction in Genesis 1 and 2 was never intended to stop there. God called Adam and Eve to extend the boundaries of the garden to the ends of the earth. "God blessed them; and God said to them, 'Be fruitful and multiply, and fill the earth, and subdue it,'" (Gen. 1:28). This was the labor of mankind: to expand God's dominion on the earth for His presence to dwell with all of creation.

Adam abdicated his priestly role when he failed to protect the sanctuary from the serpent. Even though Adam had been authorized to reign over the serpent, he succumbed to Satan's deception and allowed him to defile the sanctuary of Eden. G.K. Beale remarks, "When Adam failed to guard the temple by sinning and letting in a foul serpent to defile the sanctuary, he lost his priestly role, and the cherubim took over the responsibility of 'guarding' the Garden temple."

THIS WAS THE LABOR OF MANKIND: TO EXPAND GOD'S DOMINION ON THE EARTH FOR HIS PRESENCE TO DWELL WITH ALL OF CREATION.

The original sin of Adam resulted in not just the corruption of their personal intimacy with the Lord, but also their authority within God's temple-city. Adam's actions defiled Eden, God's temple-city and the dwelling place of His presence. Their disobedience broke their communion, resulting in their expulsion from the garden. God stationed two cherubim as the replacement guardians "to guard the way to the tree of life" (Gen. 3:24).

We see parallels in later tabernacles memorializing these two cherubim. In Moses' tabernacle there were stationed on either side of the ark of the covenant two cherubim in the Holy of Holies. These angels were reminders of what had been lost and what ultimately would be restored.

Similar parallels and patterns can be noted throughout the metanarrative of scripture: God's desire to rest with humankind, man and woman's priestly roles in the temple, and where God would come and go to meet with mankind. This established design of rest is thematic throughout the Bible, and the primary purpose for God's temple-city.

THE COMING TEMPLE-CITY OF GOD

The Bible ends the way it begins. The tabernacle of God we see in Eden is mirrored in the final chapters of Revelation. "And I heard a loud voice from the throne, saying, 'Behold, the tabernacle of God is among the people, and He will dwell among them, and they shall be His people, and God Himself will be among them'" (Rev. 21:3).

Eden's original purpose and God's original intent for all creation will finally be fulfilled. The garden city that was lost will one day be restored in the New Jerusalem. Revelation 21:1 through 22:5 details the temple that is to come.

> The new heavens and earth in Revelation 21:1–22:5 are now
> described as a temple because the temple—which equals
> God's presence—encompasses the whole earth because of

the work of Christ. At the very end of time, the true temple will come down from heaven and fill the whole creation (as Rev 21:1– 3, 10 and 21:22 affirm). Revelation 21:1 commences, as we have seen, with John's vision of a "new heaven and new earth" followed by his vision of the "new Jerusalem descending from heaven" (v. 2), and then he hears a "great voice" proclaiming that "the tabernacle of God is with men, and he will tabernacle with them . . ."[7]

This new city will fully redeem the purpose and plan for the original temple-city of Eden. The defilement of humankind's disobedience will be fully redeemed and paradise, communion with God, will be restored. God will make all things new once again. The Creator committed to His design and desire will fulfill His plan. Warren Wiersbe's commentary on Revelation 21 depicts this restoration:

In this new creation, God reverses all the tragedies that sin brought to the original creation. The old heaven and earth were plunged into judgment, this new heaven and earth glisten with perfection. Eden had an earthly river (Gen. 2:10– 14); but here we have a wonderful heavenly river. The tree of life in Eden was guarded after man sinned (Gen. 3:24); but here the heavenly tree of life is available to God's people. The curse was pronounced in Gen. 3:14–17; but now there is no more curse. Adam and Eve were forced to leave the original paradise and labor for their daily bread; but here men serve God and see His face in perfect fellowship. When the first man and woman sinned, they became slaves and lost

_____

[7] Beale, Eden, *The Temple, and the Church's Mission in the New Creation*, 25

their kingship; but v. 5 indicates that this kingship will be regained, and we shall reign with Christ forever! The present creation is not God's final product. It is groaning and travailing under the bondage of sin (Rom. 8:18–23). But one day, God will usher in His new creation, and we will enjoy perfect liberty and fullness of life forever.[8]

The plan of redemption will be fully realized when God's original tabernacle is restored. This restoration will redeem the earth's created purpose and design. The Edenic temple-city will see its fulfillment in the New Jerusalem. At that time and in that place, God's design for God's desire will be complete. The eternal resting place for both God and His people will be on a new earth in His temple-city.

WHEN JESUS RESTED

It is fascinating that Jesus had no place to rest His head while He ministered on earth. While walking the earth in the flesh, the word of God tabernacled among us and yet, by His own admonition, had no place to lay His head. The inference is that Jesus was homeless. The Son of Man did not have a home. After all, foxes live in holes and birds live in nests, but the Son of Man does not have a place to call home.

The common interpretation of this verse is that Jesus was a nomad. He moved about, passing through, not wanting a home, nor claiming a home. He was a man of simplicity, vowing to live impoverished and clinging to nothing material for He was in the world but not of it. While these

---

[8] Wiersbe, Warren W. 1992. *Wiersbe's Expository Outlines on the New Testament.* Wheaton, Ill.: Victor Books. Pg 2592.

descriptions of Jesus are fine to take away from this verse, I see a deep longing unfulfilled and exposed in the heart of Jesus.

The word for "lay" (as in, "lay His head") in the Greek is *klino*; it means "to bow, lay, or rest." Jesus had no place to *klino* His head. However, I believe this was a part of Jesus's mission. He was going to establish a body for His head to rest. The work of redemption was unto God establishing a people who would be defined by this reality—the headship of Jesus.

Jesus uttered the final words of His earthly ministry while on the cross. The "it is finished" cry from Calvary was a declaration of accomplishment. The one sent from heaven to earth finished the assignment by atoning for mankind's sin. The breach was restored through Jesus taking on sin and death. He who knew no sin had become the very thing He was an enemy of (2 Cor. 5:21). He took on sin and its wages, identifying fully with the fallenness of man as God and man.

This utterance was total surrender and submission to the Father's will. From here, the Holy Spirit would be sent from the Father to raise Jesus' lifeless body back to life. He would conquer sin, death, and the grave through this offering.

What I find fascinating in John's account of the cross is that he uses the word *klino*. This word is in relation to Jesus's head AGAIN. The head that Jesus had described as homeless now has a home—His redeemed bride. John uses *klino*, the exact word to describe Jesus's head after He says His final words, "It is finished." With that, He bowed (*klino*) His head and gave up His spirit.

Upon finishing the work of the cross, in death, Jesus *klinoed* (rested, laid, bowed) His head. It was not until the finished work of Calvary that the Son of Man's head could rest on the earth. This is a crucial part to understanding the plan of redemption through the work of salvation.

Like day seven of creation, God again is found resting (*klino*) after His work is completed. This time He was not resting from the work of creation; He was resting from the work of salvation to redeem creation. The work of salvation at Calvary is unto the restoration of all that was lost in Eden. Just as Adam was created to live in the rest of God, new believers are born into the rest of Jesus's completed work of salvation.

THE HEAD OF THE BODY, HIS CHURCH

Jesus is now the head of His body, the church. He who had no place to lay His head now has a body for His headship to rest upon. This headship should be the defining mark of His body, the church. We should be known for His leadership. In fact, it's what makes us His body, all members with one Head. Abiding in the finished work of salvation is our entry to abiding in His rest. He will not strive against us or force His way to the top. He is humble and lowly. He is honoring and submissive to our desires and, if He is our desire, He is ready and willing to manifest His presence to us.

Unfortunately, I believe Jesus has few places to *klino* His head today. Although it's one of His greatest desires, we as His body become distracted with doing so much for Him, rather than setting a time, place, and intention for His presence to come.

We as the church today should give the world a foretaste of the rest of Jesus, the headship and leadership of His presence. Jesus said, "It is to your advantage that I am leaving; for if I do not leave, the Helper will not come to you; but if I go, I will send Him to you" (John 16:7). We know the "Helper" is the Holy Spirit of God. And when the Spirit comes, we experience the manifest presence of God's leadership on the earth today.

He desires to manifest Himself intentionally, willfully, and directly. The manifest presence of Jesus is tangible, experiential, and transformational. While there is nowhere we can be that He is not, we must understand that He desires to show up.

As in Eden, He desires to make Himself known intimately and personally, in unique spaces and times. He desires to be welcomed, acknowledged, thanked, adored, worshiped, and received. This reception is more than religious protocol and routine. This reception is a surrender and submission to His headship. He, who we welcome as the guest of honor, desires to be the host—to commune with us in His rest. He, who we welcome into our homes (personal and corporate), desires to make those homes His resting place.

> HE, WHO WE WELCOME AS THE GUEST OF HONOR, DESIRES TO BE THE HOST—TO COMMUNE WITH US IN HIS REST.

Chapter 3

HIS PRESENCE IS PRIORITY

As we have stated, the metanarrative of the Bible is God desiring a dwelling place on the earth. In the garden He dwelled with Adam and Eve, and in Revelation 22 His tabernacle will be dwelling among men on the earth. If we long to base our lives, leadership, and churches on scriptural truth, we must create a space and prioritize our time unto God as the central focus of our gatherings. Him dwelling among us is His desire, and therefore Him dwelling among us must be our goal. His presence resting upon a group of people is what must define His House—the modern-day church.

What does it look like for His manifest presence to come dwell upon communities regularly gathering? It will involve many of the things that we do today, but a shift in focus—that everything we do is through, in, and unto Him. We must get delivered from ourselves, and His presence is the very thing that will prune us. As the Lord makes His bride ready, the presence of God will be rediscovered, revered, and necessary. We are an end-time generation. God's manifest presence coming to earth is a critical puzzle piece that will prepare the bride and usher in our Bridegroom's return.

This is how it all started in Acts 2 and where it will end in Revelation 22. In Acts 2, the Holy Spirit was sent from heaven upon the 120 gathered in the upper room. In Revelation 22, that same Spirit will propel Jesus from heaven to earth to answer the cry of millions of believers on earth, desperate for His salvation and lovesick for His return. The way it began is how it will end. The Holy Spirit will marry heaven and earth through us becoming one with Jesus, just as He prayed in John 17: Him in us and us in Him, just as He is in the Father. Heaven and earth will become one, all under His reign.

As this becomes more of a reality to us, and especially church leaders, our priorities will shift. We will transition from a focus on people to a person, from the presence of masses to the presence of one man. Our desire will not be to influence the earth but to move heaven.

Rick Joyner asked a question in his book Apostolic Ministry that forever changed my approach to pastoring. He asked what it would look like if we built communities that first attracted God and not people. What would it look like if we made His presence as the priority for everything we do as a church community?

This shift will be incredibly uncomfortable for most of the church, and especially for church leaders. For far too long, we have been lured into a consumerist mentality that focuses on feeding people whatever they communicate they want—better music, a good show, an entertaining sermon, kids' jungle gyms, craft coffee, and plenty of parking and seating. We measure success by what we can accomplish and how pleased our congregants are. We have measured growth and success by resources and people and have wrongly homed in on the ever-changing appetites of others, feeding them our best products and most educated, charismatic, and polished personalities. This must change.

Much of what is a priority today will not be a priority in the future. Once we get delivered from ourselves, including our flesh that prefers the ease and comfort of a scheduled program, we will be less driven by a clock, people-pleasing, attracting a crowd, or even passing the offering baskets.

I have seen this shift in our local church body over time, but it has indeed taken time. Corporately, we share a common goal in our gatherings: to create a space for His presence to come, and once He does, we together hone our awareness of His leadership. It has been laborious, awkward, and confusing at times. It can turn people off, seem to take too long, or even feel chaotic, especially to a newcomer.

I don't want my schedule or leadership decisions to be dictated by others and their various opinions and preferences. I want to live my life— every aspect of being a husband, father, pastor, and leader—hinged on His word, submitted to His leadership, tethered to His grace, and fueled by His Spirit. This is what it means for me to rightly respond to the manifestation of God's presence. Our staff and church body are continually learning how to do this individually and corporately.

Biblically, there are prescriptive measures to rightly approach God and host His presence when He comes. We will dive more into those in later chapters, but as we learn how to rightly approach and respond to Him, our focus will shift from ourselves to Him. And He is so much better to look at. "He is altogether lovely" (Song of Sol. 5:16), and "We know that when He appears, we will be like Him, because we will see Him just as He is" (1 John 3:2).

His presence is the best thing for me, for us, for everyone. I have learned that the presence of Jesus will disrupt and re-organize everything unto one thing—unto Him. He has desires, burdens, longings. He has joys and sorrows He longs to share with us. He has things He wants to do, and I have seen over and over again that it is always better, more fun, wilder, and more powerful than anything I could have planned.

The fruit of His presence manifests when we are postured to receive Him and all that He brings. I have heard it said that faith is spelled R-I-S-K. It is risky, especially as a leader, to push through all that is awkward and uncomfortable and be dependent on His presence coming, but there is a great reward in the pursuit. "And without faith it is impossible to please Him, for the one who comes to God must believe that He exists, and that He proves to be One who rewards those who seek Him" (Heb. 11:6).

THE LORD IS THERE

The book of Ezekiel is a book that is complex and, at times, challenging to comprehend. The framework of the prophet's journey over the book takes us from judgment to restoration. The book begins with a people who were hard in heart, cut off, rebellious, and ultimately exiled far from God. The book ends detailing the renewal of a new man, a new temple, and a new city. It is incredibly descriptive in what is to come to the earth in the last days, and specifically in the last eight chapters.

In the last chapter, the prophet takes a step back and scrolls out from the details of all the previous chapters, where he has described at length the various ways restoration will happen to the city of God. Like a Google map, Ezekiel pans out from the city streets, and intricate details of the temple, to a broad view of all that has happened.

He gives the dimensions of the coming city, its various gates and walls and specific measurements. In the last verse, the final words of the book give us the name of the city he has just described. This name would be the ultimate description of all that has been built and all that is to come. I want to draw your attention to the last verse in the book of Ezekiel: "The city shall be eighteen thousand cubits all around; and the name of the city from that day shall be, 'The Lord is there'" (Ezek. 48:35).

The name of the city is JEHOVAH-SHAMMAH, "The Lord Is There." What a beautiful reality—the Lord is there. It's as if Ezekiel is saying the ultimate description of the place, the marker for everyone who lives there and anyone visiting, would be summed up in those four words. It is the distinctive and distinguishing indicator of this region from any other place—the presence of the Lord. THE LORD IS THERE.

I am certain the same is true of heaven and what makes heaven, heaven—the Lord is there. The streets of gold, the sea of glass, the myriads of angels, the elders and living creatures all point to and are zeroed in on the King of heaven, the Lamb that was slain, the One on the throne. Without question, all of heaven is aware of the Lord's presence. There would be no obstacles or distractions to deter an awareness of His being. In heaven, we will be aware of nothing else but this one reality—the Lord is there.

> THE LORD IS THERE.

This is the ultimate answer to the Lord's prayer in Matthew 6, "Thy kingdom come, thy will be done, on earth as it is in heaven." This will be fulfilled one day, in a city called The Lord Is There. Jesus and His Kingdom are coming to the earth, and upon His return, heaven and earth will be made one. The glory of the Lord will cover the earth like the waters cover the sea. This is a scriptural promise and will mark the beginning of a new age for all mankind.

At that time, those four words will be experienced by everyone—the Lord is there. It will be a universal reality experienced by all of creation.

We will not question who He is, what He is like, what He desires, and what His reign is, because we will be one with Him. This is the ultimate reality, destiny, and goal for Jesus, and us, His bride. It will be the fulfillment of His temple—a resting place for Him to dwell.

OMNIPRESENCE VS. GOD'S MANIFEST PRESENCE

You can look outside or watch the news and know that this is obviously not yet a reality for all today. In fact, it is not even the highest value or reality for His people today. This is changing though, and in order to welcome the shift, and ready our hearts and lives, we must understand the difference between God's omnipresence and His manifest presence. There is a very distinct difference.

The omnipresence is for everyone. God is everywhere, at any time, with anyone. David said in Psalm 139:7-8, "If I go to the highest of heights you are there. If I make my bed in sheol, you are there. Where can I go to escape your presence?" This is the omnipresence of God and is understood and accepted by most Christians.

In addition, for the believer, there is the inward reality of His presence. This is the promise that every born-again believer has become a temple of God. The Spirit of the Lord dwells inside of us when we put our faith in Jesus. This inhabitation of His Spirit is experienced through the fruits of the Spirit, most notably the peace, joy, and love of God. It is an inward knowing that He is inside of me, leading me into truth, guiding me in His ways.

The universal omnipresence of God, and the indwelling presence of the Holy Spirit are different from the manifest presence. The manifest presence of God is an external reality and outward expression of His nearness, best described by Jesus in John 14 when He said, "He will remain in you and be with you." The "with you" presence of God is the external manifest presence of God around you.

All these expressions are real, biblical, and true to God's nature and character. Yet, there are unique differences to all of them. Specifically in the atmosphere of the manifest presence of God, the Lord is tangibly perceived. This experience moves us beyond the theoretical reality of His omnipresence to the transformational reality of His being present—in person, with thoughts, feelings, words, ideas and action.

This is not a universal reality always happening, but a selective one initiated by Him at a specific time and place. Not always, but there is usually a level of intentionality and desire to encounter the presence of God that invites Him to manifest. Through praise, worship, and prayer we become aware of His especially near presence. He moves from being an otherly and Almighty King to a highly personal and near Father, comforter, and counselor. He is no longer an abstract idea but a supernatural reality that we can sense, know, encounter, and engage.

A.W. Tozer in his classic treatise The Pursuit of God explains, "The presence and the manifestation of the presence are not the same. There can be one without the other. God is here when we are wholly unaware of it. He is manifest only when and as we are aware of His presence."

> HE MOVES FROM BEING AN OTHERLY AND ALMIGHTY KING TO A HIGHLY PERSONAL AND NEAR FATHER, COMFORTER, AND COUNSELOR.

This awareness is our greatest need today. Frank Hartly says, "The reason the church is in crisis today is because we have settled for the omnipresence rather than for the manifest presence of God." If this statement is true, then we have some re-learning and re-prioritizing to do. And by that, I mean re-penting. We must change our way of thinking in regard to church growth, influence, success, fruit, and "measurables." Everything boils down to our understanding of this one thing.

I have a desperate conviction to lead from this place and usher my church family and the greater global church into an awareness of hosting His presence. This reality is what marked the 120 in the original upper room gathering in Acts. This reality will mark the end time church awaiting the return of the Lord. Where the church began is where it will end—marked by His presence. I want to be in the generation waiting, eagerly expecting the return of Jesus to earth. I want to establish the realities to come by learning to rightly host His manifest presence now. It is the practical preparation for us as the welcoming party of Jesus's return.

The preparation of this welcoming party will involve many of the activities we are doing today—preaching, worship, discipleship, and evangelism are incredibly important and impactful. But these activities must be secondary to the primary reality of His manifest presence. In fact, the presence of God will enhance and empower every one of these activities to be a grace, not a striving or religious obligation. We will realize we cannot do any Christian activity or discipline effectively without His manifest presence.

I have seen some of the hardest of hearts, antagonists of the gospel, and haters of God and His people melt in environments when He is present. He gives ears to hear and eyes to see. He removes veils of unbelief and offense. He rescues and saves to completely (Heb. 7:25).

LET HIM HUG YOU

One of the logistical challenges we faced having church in the homosexual neighborhood of Dallas happened every year during the pride parade. UPPERROOM was on a main thoroughfare in a very urban area. The pride parade is usually held on a Sunday with peripheral celebrations occurring all day.

As our UPPERROOM families were walking into church, often intoxicated parade-goers were walking through our parking lot holding all sorts of less-than-family-friendly signs and wearing all sorts of expressive outfits. Cowboy chaps with nothing underneath was a popular one.

Our sanctuary had windows all around, so even during worship we could easily see all the excitement ensuing outside. One year, after the evening service and the pride parade, a man approached me to introduce himself. He said he had been coming to UPPERROOM for several weeks and sitting in the back corner. He said that he loved to come sit and listen to people sing to Jesus. "When you all sing, I feel like someone is hugging me."

He said, "Last year, I was on one of the floats in the parade. I was a very well-known drag queen." He had left the homosexual lifestyle and wanted to know if we had a program for "someone like him."

"Yes!" I replied enthusiastically, "Keep sitting in that corner and let Him hug you while we sing."

You see, God's presence was touching the heart of this man in such a tangible way. He knew what the Bible said about homosexuality but had not personally encountered the God of the Bible. Sure, we can all agree that God's presence is everywhere, but for this man, God was especially close, revealing Himself in a way that no teaching, podcast, or program could. That is the manifest presence of Jesus.

THE HOLY SPIRIT

The biggest question is how do we live our lives unto this end? How does the manifest presence of Jesus become central to us as disciples and leaders, as well as corporately in our churches?

The presence of Jesus is the only way to truly know Jesus. We need one to know the other. It is a humbling reality—you cannot know Jesus outside of the Holy Spirit. The Spirit must reveal Jesus to each of us in order for us to know Him.

It is within that reality I refer to the Holy Spirit as the presence of God. For me, it makes Him (the person of the Holy Spirit) more relatable. For too long, I related to the Holy Spirit as heaven's subcontractor. I knew Him by His work. I only saw Him as one who worked for the Father and the Son. I did not view Him as a unique part of the Trinity.

I don't know what your understanding of God's presence is today. Depending on your church background, your understanding of, and relationship to, the Holy Spirit will vary drastically. He is more than a giver of supernatural gifts, more than a tree that bears good fruits, and more than the Pentecostal-type manifestations—although He may exhibit all the aforementioned.

The Holy Spirit is a person. His presence is the presence of God on the earth. Where the Ark of the Covenant was a token representation of God's presence with the Israelites in their day, the Holy Spirit has now become the representation of God's presence for us. The Holy Spirit reveals Jesus and *is* the Spirit of Jesus. Paul refers to the Holy Spirit inside of us as the "Spirit of His Son" (Gal. 4:6).

We can learn a lot about Jesus in the scriptures. We can read about His life, ministry, teachings, miracles, and the cross. But without the

Holy Spirit etching onto our hearts the revelation of Jesus, we will simply grow in knowledge and not relationship. We will become more informed about Him instead of actually being in relationship with Him.

MORE CAUGHT THAN TAUGHT

"Oh, I get it now...this is the presence."

A longtime friend said that phrase to me one night at the UPPER-ROOM. It was a great moment of breakthrough for both me and him because for way too long, when he heard me talk about the UPPERROOM, he had no idea what I was talking about.

I would use words like "the presence" or "ministering to Jesus" or "rightly responding to Him" in our services, and he really thought I was crazy. He was an astute Bible student, a lover and disciple of Jesus, yet He had no grid for God's manifest presence on the earth today.

He believed the Spirit was deposited in us to bear fruit in our lives, help us understand scripture, and possibly endow gifts to God's people. Every believer needed to approach this topic with reverence and sobriety because many have been led astray by "abuses" and "extremes" regarding the Holy Spirit. In his mind, I, and the people I led at UPPERROOM, definitely could have fit in some of those unhealthy categories.

Yet, on this particular night, he caught what was happening. It was something he had to experience himself to understand. I believe this is true of the presence of Jesus: we must experience it to understand it. Some have said, "It is more caught than taught," and I would agree.

Although you can teach on Him, memorize verses about Him, and even pray to Him, these approaches to the Holy Spirit all fall short of a true knowledge of and dynamic relationship with Him. We need to understand and value the Holy Spirit for who the Bible says He is—God on the earth today. He is sent from the Father, by request of the Son, to reveal God to us. The Holy Spirit is a person with thoughts, feelings, and a will.

When this reality turns into conviction, the presence of the Holy Spirit will be valued for what it truly is—the very person of God manifesting on earth. The presence will not be sought for an emotional feeling, external demonstration, or manifestation of a gift or supernatural power. The presence will be valued for God's arrival and nearness. We will start to believe and know that the presence of Jesus can and does transform lives. And we will learn that how we respond to His presence is ultimately how we respond to Him in every aspect of our lives.

Preaching, singing, and gathering will be unto this end: His presence bringing His leadership and His Kingdom to earth. People will gather to sit at the feet of Jesus, together tending to this beautiful man. We will begin to see that our primary ministry is not to people, but to this glorious and worthy person who, when given the space to manifest and lead, will encounter, and minister to, every person.

> THE OVERFLOW OF OUR MINISTRY TO HIM WILL BE HIS MINISTRY TO US.

He is better at teaching, convicting, encouraging, and healing than you or I ever will be. Let's set a table, invite Him to come, and when He comes, let us host His presence. When we rightly respond to Him, He becomes the host and feeds everyone at the table. The overflow of our ministry to Him will be His ministry to us. Every other activity and church program must be fueled by this pure, first-love, bridal ministry.

MARKED BY HIS PRESENCE

Proverbs 24:3 (NIV) says, "By wisdom a house is built, and through understanding it is established." Godly wisdom is oftentimes foolishness to men. In planting the UPPERROOM the Lord taught us repeatedly about His wisdom in building, rather than our own. We know that unless He builds the house, the laborers will labor in vain. Therefore, it is crucial to find His wisdom for building His house in our hour.

His wisdom led us in the most unconventional church plant. Practically everything the books say to do for effective and successful church planting, we seemed to do the opposite. I am certain many of you have heard of the *Purpose Driven Church* by Rick Warren. This was the precursor to the bestseller, *Purpose Driven Life*. It was, and probably still is, the most popular "how to" guide to planting an attractional church, and foundational to the megachurch movement in our current era. I had not read this book until about a year ago, when I felt the Lord prompt me to read it. When I did, I was shocked at how many of the principles the UPPERROOM, and consequently I, as the leader, violated in planting the church.

There are many resources that ascribe worship should only last a certain length of time and only use songs that transcend into culture in order for lost people to connect. These assimilation models take people strategically through a process where they would go from unbelievers to disciples. There were programs outlined for every need and every season of life. It was comprehensive and very impactful, and obviously effective. Yet, the UPPERROOM did not adhere to Warren's or anyone else's prescribed and proven techniques.

Again, everything about launching the UPPERROOM was such a challenge because it was foolish according to the ways that seemed right, the ways I would have been more comfortable with. From not creating a website, to not planning community or ministry opportunities, He was really concerned about us focusing on the one thing—His presence. I knew He wanted this church to be marked by Him and Him alone; this was His story that we were invited into. This was not about my story, my calling, or gifting.

Years ago, a man told me a vision he had of a crystal glass with a light beaming through the crystal. It was translucent with the brightest, clearest light beaming through it. There were myriad colors radiating from the light and hitting the crystal. He described this as the glory of God, and said to me, "the Lord is looking for leaders who will not put their fingerprints on the crystal. He is looking for those that won't put their markings on His move. It will take diligence, humility, and extreme obedience." I began to realize then, and continue to remind myself, that He wants to bring forth a nameless and faceless move of God that is marked by Him and His presence alone.

"Who is the senior pastor?" is one of the most common questions I hear humming around our church community. We have a team of teachers that are in rotation at our campuses, and I only teach about 60 percent of the weekends, so it is not uncommon for someone to visit the UPPERROOM and I am not the one teaching.

Additionally, we have sixteen worship leaders who lead any given weekend service. But the one common and consistent element in every one of our gatherings, and what I believe has marked our community since the beginning, is the presence of the Lord. His presence has been our aim and remains our greatest reward.

The manifest presence of Jesus is the answer for our hour, as we believe He can and does transform anything and anyone. We have seen Him transform prodigals, marriages, racists, misogynists, addicts, the religious, broken, sick, and proud. So many of our meetings are marked with awe and wonder, knowing that only God could have done what takes place. I am not limiting this to the miraculous, although we have seen miracles happen, but ordinary moments that become supernaturally marked by the tangible manifestation of God's presence in and among us.

George Otis is a seasoned researcher of revival and how it impacts culture. His ministry has documented and validated several moves of God in our lifetime. In the early days of UPPERROOM, George was visiting a friend in Dallas and attended a weekend service. During the time of worship, the Holy Spirit came so beautifully, and I sensed His desire to focus on the nations. I leaned into His leadership and was prompted on this specific night to call up anyone present who was born outside of the U.S. Surprisingly, from the approximately 400 people present, there were at least fifty nations represented.

A spirit of intercession came into the room and people were gripped with a global burden to see God save the nations. We had tapped into His unique burden for our gathering that night, and great faith and unity erupted corporately as we prayed. After a significant time interceding for the nations, I gave a salvation call out of Revelation 7:9 that every tribe and every tongue will confess His Lordship, and a number of people gave their lives to the Lord. I never got to my planned sermon, yet it was a beautiful night that beat any message I could have delivered. His presence always has a better word.

George approached me afterwards to introduce himself and tell me more about his ministry. He mentioned how unique of a gathering and community ours was and that he hoped one day to document the impact we are having upon our city. I was humbled to say the least.

As George and I were ending our conversation I asked him a question that had been nagging me as he was talking about the revivals he researched. I knew that he had seen moves of God in several nations across the globe, and I knew he had witnessed commonalities in each of them. So, I asked him what he had seen was the one common denominator in every move of God he had studied? Without hesitation he said, "It's a small consensus of people radically committed to one thing." I knew that one thing for our community was and always would be the presence of Jesus. At all costs, our community would create a space and place where His presence would be paramount to anything and anyone, and most importantly, that His leadership would be paramount to mine.

> AT ALL COSTS, OUR COMMUNITY WOULD CREATE A SPACE AND PLACE WHERE HIS PRESENCE WOULD BE PARAMOUNT TO ANYTHING AND ANYONE, AND MOST IMPORTANTLY, THAT HIS LEADERSHIP WOULD BE PARAMOUNT TO MINE.

In Psalm 27:4 David said, "One thing I have asked from the Lord, that I shall seek: that I may dwell in the house of the Lord all the days of my life, to behold the beauty of the Lord and to meditate in His temple." David's one desire was to behold the presence of the Lord all the days of his life. I am convinced this one thing is the thing for our day—the only thing. Every other thing is secondary to this primary pursuit of Him.

We embarked upon it with one weekly meeting every Sunday night. This primary pursuit has now been multiplied to meetings every morning, noon, and night happening seven days a week at UPPERROOM. People who have been trained, equipped, and given their lives to this one goal: hosting the presence of God.

Our question was not how to impact and gather people or influence our region. Our mandate was to create a community that is first and foremost attractive to the Lord. From the beginning of UPPERROOM and to this day, I am continually asking what would a resting place for His presence look like on the earth today? I long for every gift, resource, and energy to be focused on creating a resting place for the Lord's presence to dwell.

DECONSTRUCTION UNTO A PERSON

For too long, we have been a people of many things. But our agendas, our platforms, our influence, and our vision will no longer sustain us in the hour ahead. Only Jesus will sustain us. We have to burn every other ship and every other means we have sought to sustain us. He and His presence with us must be the distinguishing mark of His people. He will be in us, and He will be with us, and His nearness is our good.

The tragedy today is that a generation is deconstructing the very constructs intended to point us to a person. Churches, the scriptures, faith leaders, and even the deconstruction of faith as we have known it is a worthy endeavor when it allows us to see the object of our faith more clearly. The questioning and paring that both seasoned believers and many young people are doing today should not scare or intimidate us. They are seeking, and they don't need to find a hip program, good band, or entertaining church service, they need to find the man of Jesus, the presence of the Holy Spirit, and the love of the Father. He is the answer to our question and the point of our faith. As our traditional constructs become questioned and discarded, it can actually be good and healthy—and unto the revelation of Jesus, the true object of our faith. In my experience with deconstruction, it is incredibly difficult to deconstruct a person.

We have built too much scaffolding around Jesus, and the scaffolding should come down. Scaffolding is unto the establishment of a building. It is used to help support something in its construction phase. I believe the deconstruction of religion that is happening right now is an opportunity for the actual person of Jesus to be seen and the tangible presence of the Lord to be encountered. Deconstruction can be a reintroduction to the Jesus we thought we knew, but attempted to leave when churches, programs, and activities were devoid of His presence. It is my prayer that the deconstruction commonly occurring today will serve as a personal reintroduction to a radical relationship with the One who is alive and near.

We know from scripture that everything that can be shaken will be shaken. I believe the deconstruction among today's younger generation is shaking what the church has offered up until this point. The religious scaffolding must crumble if we want to see the person of Jesus rightly. We will receive the unshakable Kingdom and the knowledge of the true King when the scaffolding falls away and we see and receive Him as He truly is.

Jesus is the point—not the sermon, not the response of the congregants, not the size of the altar call or tithe. Jesus is our purpose, pursuit, and goal. May each preaching, ministry, offering, or response only be accompanied, birthed, and sustained, by the person of Jesus. He is truly our all in all. We need nothing more and cannot settle for anything less.

Leaders will no longer be admired for their polished preaching, but for their humility to rightly respond to His presence. They will be respected for their willingness to become unknown when He arrives—to give Him the stage and agenda. He will be preeminent, and His name will be above any other name. This will be most effective with a plurality of leaders, partnering together to tend to and minister to Him and lead others corporately in ministry to Him. Many of the same activities that we do today will still occur, but it will be with an awareness that everything is unto the one thing. The mark of leadership in the coming days will not be one's ability to influence people but move heaven; it will be in the humility of being a follower whose eyes, speech, and entire life are fixated on the best leader, Jesus.

Chapter 4

THE FIRST COMMANDMENT

Jesus is the perfect revelation of God. God, who for centuries has been interpreted through lesser revelations, has chosen to define Himself through one person: Jesus Christ. The basis of our faith as Christians is that Jesus is the highest revelation of God. My thoughts about God have to be found in the person of Jesus. If God had a face, hands, and feet; if God could talk, walk, and engage with us, what would He be like?

All of these questions can be answered in the life of Jesus. We do not have to interpret God through any other means. You do not have to look to the stars in the heavens, the glorious mountains, or seas; although creation reveals God, creation is not God.

Jesus ends all questions surrounding the mystery of who God is. The word of God took on flesh and became a man. Any idea or thought that you have about God must be found in the life and revelation of Jesus. Jesus is the exact representation of God to us today, and if we want to know God, we must get to know Jesus.

It is crucial for us to understand this because when we read the Gospels, we have direct insight and revelation to what God says, thinks, and does. When Jesus is asked a question, we have God's answer. I shout for joy thinking of the humility and profound reality that the infinite un-created God became an embryo. The eternal and timeless One became bound by flesh, hours, and days.

In our hour, people are attempting to redefine Jesus. Culture is attempt-ing to make Jesus into something that He is not. They will embrace His di-vinity but not His deity. Jesus will be who you want Him to be, not who He said He was. The post-Christian culture is attempting to water down the truths that Jesus made about Himself: He claimed He was God; He claimed He was Messiah; He was the Lamb sent from heaven to remove the sins of the world. There is NO other name on the earth by which we are saved.

Jesus is the most polarizing person to ever walk the planet. The state-ments that He made and the life that He lived force us to accept or deny this reality. There is no middle ground when it comes to the life that He lived and the words that He said.

FIRST COMMANDMENT

With that as a backdrop, it is important to hear what Jesus reveals about God with His own words. When a teacher of the law asked Jesus what was the most important, or greatest, commandment, Jesus did not miss a beat. When God tells us what's most important to God, we would do well to pay attention.

"You shall love the Lord your God with all your heart, and with all your soul, and with all your mind. This is the great and foremost com-mandment." He continued, "The second is like it, 'You shall love your neighbor as yourself.' Upon these two commandments hang the whole

Law and the Prophets" (Matt. 22:36-40). Not only is this the greatest commandment, but also everything else He desires from humanity is implicated in these two all-encompassing commandments.

This answer is simple yet profound. Here we find great insight to the personality and heart of God. This command is not a demand—because no one can demand love. It reveals what He values. This is insight into what He desires from the earth—and ultimately what He desires from you and me. He has made Himself vulnerable by expressing His desire. He desires love, all our love, even when He knows all our weaknesses.

Please catch the weightiness of this reality. Little insignificant you—walking on the earth and attempting to find purpose and meaning to life—loving big omnipotent, omniscient, omnipresent Him—who is surrounded by thousands of angels, the four living creatures, all the nations will acknowledge Him—and His greatest desire is you loving Him. In His eyes, you are so significant and valuable. Your love moves Him. Your love provokes Him. Your love stirs Him.

There is so much to be discovered in this statement. Your Creator has expressly stated the whole reason for your existence: it is here we can find our created purpose. What a relief! How is a life to be measured before the Creator? What is the mark of a life well lived? Money, success, ministry, etc.? Jesus says that the mark of a successful life is one that learned to love God. Your purpose on earth is to grow in love for the Lord. Everything else will align when this primary initiative is before you. Before your marriage, your calling, and your desires, this one thing will define everything.

Yet, what does it actually mean to love God? I am certain that this would be up for debate and could include a number of things. Loving God is a lifetime lesson where we grow and mature in our expressions. Listen to the Spirit of God inviting you to reevaluate this commandment and how to do it. For too long, we have settled for doing things for God in the name of "loving God."

With good intention, we have believed we are loving Him by offering sacrifices to Him that focus on others and not Him. We have twisted this commandment and made it into something it was never intended to be. In the name of loving God, we are going to do a lot for God. In the name of loving God, we are going to love people. In the name of loving God, we are going to go to the nations. In the name of loving God, we are going to _____ (fill in the blank).

> FOR TOO LONG, WE HAVE SETTLED FOR DOING THINGS FOR GOD IN THE NAME OF "LOVING GOD."

Of course, it is easy to prefer these measurables, and oftentimes we ease our religiously bent consciences by doing things to "love" God. It feels good to quantify how many mission trips I have been on, how much money I have given, how many hours I have spent volunteering. We find measurable expressions of our love for Him, and we wrongly replace the first commandment with putting a priority on the second.

Loving people is not loving God. Loving God is loving God. If Jesus meant for us to equate loving others to loving God, He would not have needed to separate the two commandments. Indeed, He was clear. He said the first and greatest commandment was to love God with all that we have and all that we are.

REDEFINING MINISTRY

You have a primary ministry today. That ministry is the same as mine—every follower of Jesus has the same primary ministry. If I poll a group of active followers of Jesus and ask them "what is your ministry?" I imagine I would get a variety of answers.

People are called to the nations as missionaries; others are teachers of the scriptures; still some are called to acts of justice for the poor, widows, or orphans. There are hundreds of noble ministries today that people are truly called to fulfill, and it is their designed purpose from God. Yet, none of these ministries are your primary ministry.

There is one ministry that fuels every other ministry—it is your ministry to Him. The most important ministry we have as God's people is to minister to Him. As we love God directly, we are ministering to Him. When asked, "What's your ministry?" few people will answer "My primary ministry is the Lord Himself." Yet, this is what God desires most from us. This phrase "ministering to God" is one that is not often talked about or taught in the church today. It is so simplistic that it is provocative.

As I mentioned in chapter one, one of the most freeing (and frustrating) things God spoke to me in the early days of UPPERROOM was that He had not called me to minister to people; He had called me to first and foremost minister to Him. This completely shifted my paradigm. As a leader of His church, I had always thought that my primary call was to minister to people. I exist to minister to people and impact them for the gospel, making disciples of all nations. My energy and focus were on meeting the needs of those around me. Yet, God was telling me this was not the primary focus of my ministry and influence.

My primary ministry, your primary ministry, our primary ministry—is to minister to Jesus. It will take time, surrender, and the death of all worldly and religious standards to even begin to embrace this lifestyle. It will also, undoubtedly, be the most freeing and fulfilling pursuit of your life because it is the very reason you exist.

This is the greatest command we have been given because it is God's greatest desire. In fact, your life will be measured based upon this verse. When you stand before Him, this one thing is the most important thing.

When we obey the first commandment, we find deliverance. This deliverance will purge us from any and every other lover. As the bride of Christ, we have a natural beauty. This beauty is so attractive to the Lord and ultimately will be attractive to the world.

Today, the bride of Christ in the Western world is caked with makeup in our feeble attempt to make her appealing to the world. We are entertaining! We have something for everyone! Don't worry, we will make this as convenient as possible for you!

Meanwhile, true irresistible beauty is found in the pure and unadulterated beauty of the glory of God that He bestows on a bride who is enamored with Him. This bride has discovered that His love for her is the only makeup she will ever need. His robes of righteousness clothe her in a glory that all of creation is longing to see revealed.

THIS IS THE GREATEST COMMAND WE HAVE BEEN GIVEN BECAUSE IT IS GOD'S GREATEST DESIRE.

The world is obsessed with true love. Remember the global watch party during the royal wedding of Prince William to Kate Middleton? Or think of a wedding you have been to; when the doors of the sanctuary open, we stand and turn to see the bride on the most beautiful day of her life. Then we quickly crane our necks to see the groom. What is his reaction when he sees her, his beloved? Is he crying? Is he smiling? Seeing his bride walking toward him is a moment he has longed for.

Oh, bride of Christ! This love, this first love, is our destiny. Fall head over heels, hard in love with your Groom and trust me, the world will watch. The world will want that kind of love—the kind that makes the bride the only one in the room; the kind of love that causes a groom to weep with delight. Jesus is jealous in love for us. Can you hear Him? You don't need all that makeup, performance, glitter, or glam—I will clothe you and cover you in MY glory.

HOSTING JESUS

Now that we've established what is unequivocally the most important desire of God, let's determine how He defines great love for Him. What does it look like? Let's cast off our religious works and discover how He wants to be loved. Thankfully, we don't have to guess. Jesus provided us with a beautiful case study in which He describes someone loving Him much.

Imagine, for a moment, that you hear Jesus is in town and passing through your neighborhood. You extend an invitation, hoping to host a dinner for Him with all your friends. He is the talk of the town; everyone trying to figure out who this man is and why He is creating such a buzz amongst the region's leaders. You desire to see for yourself exactly who He is, and to your elation, He accepts your invitation and is coming to your home. I like to imagine this is typical of Jesus—He rarely, if ever, turns down an invitation when invited. He also loves a good dinner party.

You are amped. The night is approaching. Your excitement is matched by your growing curiosity about meeting the One everyone was talking about. You wonder what you should serve for dinner and which friends to invite. After all, you are about to host the most famous proclaimed prophet of your day. You have been genuine in your pursuit of God for most of your life, and your friends are in the same pursuit as you. You, along with them, have heard about Jesus and are expectant about what the night could hold.

The night arrives, and you have made all the preparations. Your anticipation only grows, as you recall the numerous stories you have heard about this proclaimed Messiah. Days earlier, Jesus was walking through your city, and He intersected a grieving widow at the funeral for her recently deceased son. Her son had died suddenly and tragically, but when Jesus touched the young boy's coffin, his lifeless body came back to life. A DEAD BOY CAME TO LIFE BECAUSE OF THIS MAN'S TOUCH! Of course, Jesus was the talk of the town, as no one had ever done such miraculous signs in your day. This Jesus will be your guest in a matter of hours.

Your friends and family arrive early to your house, all buzzing with nervous excitement. There is animated debate—some believe He is who He says He is, the Son of God. Others are skeptical, but hopeful. You are setting up a firsthand encounter with Jesus for yourself, your family, and your friends. Tonight, everyone will see for themselves who this man is and what He is like.

Jesus arrives right on time. He is not as impressive as you had imagined; He is meeker and gentler than you expected. But He is extremely present and engaging. He is listening intently and aware of everyone around Him and everything before Him. He listens more than He speaks. He asks more questions than He gives answers. He is zeroed in on everyone, and everyone is honed in on Him.

As the night gets rolling, you gather everyone around the table to formally welcome them to your house, introduce Jesus, and express your deep gratitude for His time and appearance at your home. You share the agenda for the evening, assign seats, and describe the four-course meal to be served. You put Jesus next to you at the head of the table. Your servants are ready, the wine is poured, and the first course gets under way. Everything is going according to your plan—Jesus is comfortable, your friends are impressed, and everyone is enjoying themselves.

Right before the final course, the dinner is interrupted abruptly when an uninvited guest enters your home. The first thing to catch your attention is a smell; it is the overwhelming scent of perfume—pungent and overbearing. Then you hear a collective gasp coming from your guests as they recognize who is inside the house. You still don't know who it is, but you hear a woman crying. This woman is behind you, bent over the feet of your honored guest. You can't see behind you, but as you turn to stand up, you see that the hair of this uninvited guest is covering the feet of Jesus! She is on the floor, crying, kissing and anointing Jesus's feet.

The air is sucked from the room as all your guests are in stunned silence. Suddenly, everyone is looking at you, and a sense of panic overtakes you. This woman is a prostitute! Her very appearance made it obvious. Of course, she had not been in your home before, and you did not know who she was, but her occupation and social standing are evident. As everyone is looking at you, you anxiously wonder if they are associating you with her. What if Jesus thinks I invited her? Why is a prostitute at my house? How does she know where I live? Why is she so taken with Jesus?

As you quickly try to resolve this horrific interruption to your perfect evening, you turn your attention to Jesus. Surely, He will know who this woman is and what she is doing. Surely, He will stop this shocking intrusion and put an end to the offensive attention she is displaying. This is obviously off-putting to everyone, and you assume it must be appalling to Him—a prostitute touching this holy Rabbi and revered prophet.

But you realize that Jesus is not offended. He doesn't even seem uncomfortable. She rudely interrupted the planned party, but Jesus is not concerned. He turns completely around and is no longer addressing you or your guests. His attention is wholly on this woman. His hands reach out to touch her head and He begins to softly console her as she continues to weep. It's as if He is encouraging her, accepting her display.

Your disposition turns from shock and offense to fury. You are livid to be so disrespected and ignored by your guest, and especially because of a sinner. If He knew who she was, He would ask her to leave. If He knew who she was, He would ask her to set up an appointment or find another time to meet with Him. This night is about you and your friends, not this intruder. If Jesus is truly who you think He is, surely, He would respond differently to this sinner. This is not how the night is supposed to go and Jesus is enabling it to happen. He is enabling the ruin of your dinner party!

I imagine most people read this story from the book of Luke and quickly judge Simon the Pharisee through a lens of religious pride and error. I have seen myself in Simon. Honestly, I have related to him, not because of religion or error, but because of his genuine desire to rightly host Jesus.

Think about Simon for a second. He sincerely wanted to meet with Jesus, spend time with Him, and honorably host Him. I believe he had an earnest desire to fellowship with and personally know Jesus. His approach to the Lord was the approach we all would most likely employ—friends, food, and a table for conversation and connection. Everyone at the party knew about Jesus and everyone at the party wanted to personally know Him. This is an honorable and respected desire.

Yet we see someone else who had the same desire but took a drastically different approach. This woman broke all social codes and completely crashed a private party. In the entire recounting of this story, it is amazing that she did not speak one word. However, she was by far the loudest guest that evening. She took center stage and Jesus was completely comfortable with her approaching Him in the dramatic manner she did— with her pain, her affection, and her gift.

The true and only perspective that matters is Jesus's.

JESUS'S COMMENTARY

I see a parallel to today's modern church in the story of Luke 7, where two vastly different accounts of responses to the Lord are outlined at the dinner party of Simon. I want us to see this metaphorically as believers and as churches. I believe the two responses reveal where we are and the other reveals where we are heading. With a perspective of individual followers of Jesus and church communities, we can see the existing church and the emerging church today.

> JESUS WAS COMPLETELY COMFORTABLE WITH HER APPROACHING HIM IN THE DRAMATIC MANNER SHE DID— WITH HER PAIN, HER AFFECTION, AND HER GIFT.

Every Sunday, in any given city, hundreds of believers will gather in church buildings, desiring to meet with the Lord together. It is a time and place with friends and family to gather for fellowship and connection. Jesus is always willing and ready to come meet with us, so what does He do? He comes. Jesus shows up at the designated time and place as the guest of honor in the church and community that invites Him and makes preparations for Him. He sits where He is asked and receives everything placed before Him. He humbly comes into each house and honors the authority of the host, which in our modern day is the lead pastor, elders, worship leader, etc. Isaiah 30:18 says, "He waits on high to have compassion on you," and I truly believe Jesus has anticipation for every weekly church service, excited to come and be with His bride.

As a church, we set a table, invite our friends, designate a time and place, prepare a "meal," and make preparations to host Jesus and others. He always comes when asked, takes His designated seat, and abides by all the house protocols, deferring to the host's leadership. He loves to dine with His people and His desire is for us to know Him.

Yet in verse 37 of Luke 7, we see an uninvited guest who also finds the time and place to meet with Jesus and, in her own way, prepares to meet Him. Her preparations were extensive and sacrificial. She prepared to violate all social protocols and bypass the host's agenda and seating arrangement just to meet with Jesus. She brought a costly vial of perfume (probably her entire net worth) to pour out upon His feet. This was expensive and premeditated. When she came into the party unannounced and uninvited, she did not hold back—she was looking for one person. The story says she was behind His feet where Jesus was reclining.

Her response, though different from anyone else in the room, is really important for us to study. She wets His feet with her tears, kisses His feet with her lips, and anoints Him with perfume. We could accurately surmise she has completely hijacked the dinner party, and her response to Jesus is going to affect everyone present.

Her presence initiates an inner dialogue in the host that the Bible records. Simon says to Himself, "If Jesus were a prophet, He would know what kind of woman this was that was touching Him." In essence, if Jesus was who I thought He was, He would not allow this to happen. Her response to Jesus confronts Simon's perspective of Jesus. Her right response to Jesus confronts His wrong perspective of Jesus. He does not judge the woman. He judges Jesus.

Jesus is so humble and loving and delves into a parable about thankfulness and forgiveness. For the sake of all present, Jesus puts into context why the woman is doing what she is doing—offering a sacrifice of thanksgiving to Him. Radical gratitude is the only right response to radical forgiveness.

Jesus' commentary on His experience is the most interesting detail to me. He gives Simon, and us, the readers, insight into what He experienced in Simon's home and as Simon's guest of honor. Jesus looks at the woman, but addresses Simon, "Simon, do you see this woman?" It's an obvious question that He did not need to ask. Everyone saw this woman, but not everyone saw what Jesus saw when He looked at her.

> HER RESPONSE TO JESUS CONFRONTS SIMON'S PERSPECTIVE OF JESUS. HER RIGHT RESPONSE TO JESUS CONFRONTS HIS WRONG PERSPECTIVE OF JESUS. HE DOES NOT JUDGE THE WOMAN. HE JUDGES JESUS.

"I entered your house, you gave me no water for my feet, but she has wet my feet with her tears and wiped them with her hair. You gave me no kiss, but she since the time I came in, has not ceased to kiss my feet. You did not anoint my head with oil, but she anointed my feet with perfume."

Jesus compares Simon's reception of Him to the woman's reception. He essentially says, I entered your home, and this was my experience: I received no tears, no kisses, and no oil from you. Yet, I received all of those things from her. I believe Jesus is saying, "I was ready and willing to receive all of these things from you, but you did not offer them to me." I was longing for you to rightly receive me; I was open to receive your hurt, pain, affection, gifts, and offerings. But you did not give me these things.

THE LORD DESIRES OUR PAIN, AFFECTION, AND GIFTS

Luke 7 gives us great insight into the Lord's desires. He was willing to receive the pain (tears), affections (kisses), and gifts (oil) of everyone in the room. He anticipated it. He was open. Yet, they were not. Although invited as the guest of honor, His entry was no different than anyone else. For whatever reason, they did not give Him anything upon His entry.

> I ENTERED YOUR HOME, AND THIS WAS MY EXPERIENCE: I RECEIVED NO TEARS, NO KISSES, AND NO OIL FROM YOU.

The humility and patience demonstrated in Jesus is astounding. He did not force them to give something that they were not willing to give. He honored their preparations, agenda, and response to Him. He was not mad, nor upset, but humble and present. He honored their response, but He was also not willing to forbid this woman to have a different response to Him.

There is a worshiping bride emerging that is interrupting everything in our day. I believe the people of God are learning to rightly respond to the Lord when He is invited and hosted. When we gather and invite Jesus to come, He comes. Yet, when He enters, we must learn to rightly respond to His presence. We must understand that the presence of Jesus is actually Jesus. His coming to our house should be the very mark of our house, and everything and everyone in the house should hinge on His presence.

The presence of Jesus is the most transformative power on earth today. Therefore, any protocols, plans, and programs we adopt should be unto this end—His transformative power touching earth. Beyond our giftings, schedules, strategies, sermons, and ministries, we must establish His presence as the primary priority of our gathering. When He comes by His Spirit, we must acknowledge, yield to, and rightly respond to His leadership.

> HE HONORED THEIR RESPONSE, BUT HE WAS ALSO NOT WILLING TO FORBID THIS WOMAN TO HAVE A DIFFERENT RESPONSE TO HIM.

It is not that what we are doing is wrong or not enough. But I would argue that our dinner parties need to be interrupted. Our agendas need to be hijacked because we have allowed His presence to consume our gatherings. Our familiarity with the things of God must be unto a relational encounter with the dynamic, living God.

Jesus described the woman's response in this story as one who "loves much." This is a clear example of someone practicing the first commandment. I know we could define loving God in a number of ways with various expressions, but Jesus describes her response to Him as "loving much." Her disruptive and taboo display of affection was her loving Jesus much—and I imagine that means He felt loved much. Her example serves as a prescriptive exhortation to us on how Jesus likes to be received, and how we can rightly respond in love to Him.

JESUS, OUR HOST

When Jesus is loved this way, He moves from the guest of honor at the party to the host of the party. Jesus is Lord and King. He will always come when we gather and invite Him; but in humility, He honors our approach to Him. When one rightly responds to Him, in surrender, it gives Him permission, space, and time to lead and shepherd people as only He can.

The woman's response to Jesus broke through the formalities I imagine most of us are more comfortable with. Her extravagant offering and display moved Jesus, as well as challenged the others present to receive from the Lord. This could not have been planned or orchestrated by anyone in the room, including the woman at His feet. As He received her pain, affections, and gifts, she revealed His readiness to receive any offering in any manner. Her exhibition could position everyone else in the room to rightly respond to His presence and receive from the Lord what only He could give.

In this account, Jesus only says thirteen words to the woman, and I find His words profound. He tells her, "Your sins are forgiven." It is interesting to note that she did not ask for forgiveness from Him. She did not request one thing from Him. But in her offering, she postured her heart to receive what she needed from Him. The Lord gave her exactly what she needed.

She was immoral and a sinner—everyone knew that. Yet, Jesus had the ability to change the way she viewed herself by giving her what no one else could. This gift of forgiveness would transform her eternally. If she had been sick, she would have received healing. If she were tormented by demons, she would have received deliverance. Jesus knew precisely what she needed: she needed forgiveness, and by her desperate offering and right response to His presence, she received that very thing.

When people rightly love Jesus and respond to His presence, they are positioned to receive exactly what they need, when they need it. We cannot outgive the Lord. And when we collectively love and respond to Him, we will receive exactly what we need. I am convinced this is crucial for us as His people to learn if we want the fullness of who He is and what He can do.

PAIN

There were three things the woman offered the Lord. All are significant for us to understand as we grow in loving the Lord. First, she offered Him her tears. Tears represent the pain and, at times, even despair. Throughout scripture, we see the desperate bringing their tears to the Lord as an offering, and our tears are treasured by Him. Psalm 56:8 says that God puts our tears in His bottle. He collects them and accounts for them. Psalm 126:5 says that those who sow in tears shall reap with joyful shouting. Our tears are seeds we sow, which will return a harvest of joy when we give Him all our pain and despair. Your tears are a powerful offering of love and trust to the Lord, and He will hold and treasure the brokenhearted. He receives your surrendered pain as an offering of worship. Do not think that worship is only singing happy songs; your tears anoint Him as Lord when you bring them to Him.

Recently a man approached me that had been visiting UPPER-ROOM for a few months. His family had been attending our church for several years, but he had been hesitant to come because it was young and vastly different from any context of church he had experienced before. This particular evening, he came to talk to me and tell me about his experience in our community. He told me, "I found my tears in this room." Up until that point, he had not cried in twenty-one years. He told me that when we sang to the Lord, the Holy Spirit would bring forth tears from his heart's pain and disappointment from years of hardship. He had not found a way to share his pain with the Lord until he was in an environment where it was modeled for him. He told me that, through tears, he has found freedom from a hardened heart that never knew how to fully surrender pain and hurt to the Lord. Of course, it was at that moment we both began to cry. It was beautiful.

AFFECTION

Second, the woman offered her affections. Her kisses represent her deepest emotions and desires. Emotions are so crucial for us to bring to the Lord. Many in the western church are afraid to allow environments where emotions are a trusted and honored offering to the Lord. I have heard criticism of communities being too emotional or promoting emotionalism.

We must get over this hesitation. I don't trust my emotions to lead me, but I can allow my emotions to serve and worship Him when I give them to Him and ask Him to be Lord over them. Our emotions are expressions of our reaction to people and circumstances. Depression produces emotions. Love produces emotions. Sports produce emotions. Concerts and artists produce emotions. Emotions communicate one's beliefs and values, and are healthy expressions of our passions, fears, and desires. That said, we will offer our emotions somewhere to someone; as believers, we must offer our emotions to the Lord.

We don't judge people who are emotional at weddings, funerals, sporting events, or the birth of a baby. Yet, for some reason, religion has wrongly relegated emotions as unacceptable and untrustworthy in the place of worship. The psalms give us example after example of those who bring offerings of joy, peace, love, and pain to the Lord—emotions. Worship the Lord by giving Him your emotions.

GIFTS

Lastly, we see that she brought the Lord an alabaster jar of perfume. This was an extravagant and sacrificial offering that she poured on the feet of Jesus. This was not a small or rational offering to the Lord; she wanted to give something significant and valuable. This gift is representative of her value and worth. In John 12, when Mary offers the same type of offering to the Lord, Judas remarks that the offering was a waste. It could have been sold and used to feed the poor. It was foolish and bad stewardship from an earthly perspective. Yet, this extravagant offering had eternal significance to the Lord—it was oil that would anoint His body for burial. I can only imagine how deeply it impacted the Lord's heart. These acts of extravagant gifts and offerings can only be made in faith, and out of a revelation of God as an abundant giver.

Scripture speaks of God loving a cheerful giver. He does! And like our love, He does not demand our giving, so when it is offered willingly, He loves it. Foundational biblical teaching suggests we give, at minimum, a tithe to His church. Gifts are given from the heart, and He is open to receiving whatever we desire to cheerfully give to Him. We could tell you testimony after testimony of people in our community who have given radical and sacrificial gifts, and without exception, every one of those individuals have been abundantly blessed both spiritually and financially. It is true—we really cannot outgive God.

Catch the pattern here: there is so much God is willing to receive from us that He does not require from us. He designed us to live in this intimate communion and trust with Him, but He does not require it; He longs for it. How does this story of the courageous woman in Luke 7 impact you? Where can you relate to Simon or to her?

Chapter 5

BEHOLDING JESUS

Revelation 4 and 5 are two of the most significant chapters in the Bible. Unlike any other place in scripture, these two chapters describe in detail the habitation and dwelling place of God. Similar to how you or I might prefer the mountains or the ocean, God Almighty chooses to surround Himself with a specific atmosphere—He has preferences. God gave John a glimpse into this eternal dwelling place of God

In Revelation 4, we see beauty beyond imagination surrounding Him—a dramatic display of colors and sounds. John describes an emerald rainbow, a myriad of colors, and peals of thunder and lightning around the throne. We read of the four living creatures in constant worship around the throne. We read of a great congregation surrounding the throne—wholly mesmerized and captivated by Him who is at the center.

John mentions the word "throne" thirteen times in these two chapters. We read "a throne standing," "around the throne," "near the throne," "before the throne," "encircled upon the throne," "sits upon the throne," and "between the throne." All that ever has or will exist centers around His throne. It is in this vision that John sees what men have only dreamed of seeing.

Amid all this overwhelming beauty around the throne, a scene begins to unfold before John. In Revelation 5, John is taken aback by an issue that arises in heaven. An angel proclaims, "Who is worthy to open the book and its seals?" Now, for the sake of my point, I am not going to dive too deep into what is within the seal. We will, however, focus on John's response to the question the angel posed.

He begins to weep. John actually begins to weep greatly because he knows of no one worthy to open the scroll. According to John, this was a significant problem, and he was overcome with despair—no one was found worthy anywhere in heaven, on earth, or in hell to open this scroll. This was too much for John to bear and he wept loudly in heaven. So, John, the visiting human with limited perspective, responds accordingly: with despair and hopelessness.

Imagine heaven's perspective of John for a moment. This is the place where there will be no more tears, and John is weeping. This is the place where there is no sorrow, no pain, or injustice. Yet, John's eye ducts produce actual tears from a heart that is overcome with despair because of his limited understanding.

John needs leadership. At this crucial moment, the Holy Spirit gives us insight into biblical, heavenly leadership. John cannot see beyond what he knows and understands. He is without hope. As John begins to weep in heaven, at a seemingly hopeless crisis, we see heaven's leadership beautifully modeled for us.

An elder intervenes and approaches John. He is an established authoritative overseer in heaven. This word, elder, used in Revelation 5:5 is the same word used for the governing elders of the church on earth. Strong's Concordance defines "elder" as one who presides over the assembly of people gathered, also called a bishop or presbyter. These individuals represent delegated authority called to oversee others in rank and in office. This elder in heaven is a high-ranking eternal overseer around the throne of God: a governing leader in heaven.

This elder's remarkable response to John's situation and attitude should challenge every one of us as leaders and overseers on the earth. The elder's response is two-fold: first, he corrects John's perspective. He tells him to stop weeping. It wasn't that weeping was wrong—it was that John's weeping was hindering him from seeing the greater reality. In essence, the elder is saying, "Stop doing what you're doing because it is hindering you from rightly seeing what is before you."

This elder's leadership was not harsh or mean. On the contrary, this was loving, gentle, and what any spiritual leader should be trained and equipped to do with the people they lead. The elder knew that John needed to be repositioned in mind and heart to accurately see what his sorrow was obstructing.

The elder continues to model heavenly leadership: he directs John's attention to Jesus. He says to John, "Behold!" This word "behold" means to see absolutely, or to attentively see what is most important. The elder tells John, "See the Lion that is from the tribe of Judah, the Root of David has overcome." In essence, the elder directs John, "Look up! Look at Jesus. Stop looking at the problem. Focus on the greatest reality of all realities—that Jesus Christ has overcome."

This is biblical leadership: those that first personally know how to BE-HOLD, despite what they see, feel, and think. It is from this place of personally beholding Jesus that a leader will aptly know how to position others to also behold Jesus, despite what they are seeing, feeling, and thinking. For those we lead, we are to direct their eyes to fix upon the Lamb who has overcome. We have learned to put the overcoming and overwhelming reality of Jesus' power, glory, dominion, and beauty before all things. Who He is should be the lens we see every circumstance through. An accurate understanding and awareness of Him will dominate every other thought or feeling. This culture of beholding Jesus marks heaven, and I believe it is the culture that will mark the church in the days ahead.

JUST JESUS

The beginning of the UPPERROOM community was centered upon this one thing. It was as if the Lord cornered me into this reality as a young church planter who did not choose the community God called me to plant in. I did not tell the Lord, "Please, send me there." The culture chewed me up and spat me out. I had my house broken into, my car broken into, homeless men relieving themselves in our backyard, and the list could go on.

I kept telling the Lord, "You got the wrong guy." The Lord, ever patient, kept driving me deeper into the corner, convincing me of one thing: "Michael, this is all about me. You are not here because of you—you are here because of me."

There finally came a point when I truly realized that the only thing I had was Jesus. Prior to that, I could have said Jesus was all I had—maybe even preached a great sermon about it—but my heart did not yet understand the reality or practice of it. I did not have a strategy for the neighborhood. I did not have followers. I did not have a sermon in my repertoire for the hour. All I had was Jesus. At some point, I surrendered. I died. Jesus had whittled everything down to one question He was persistently asking me: "Am I enough?"

Life has a way of doing this to all of us. It will corner you and demand that you ask this one question—is Jesus enough? It is in the corner, at rock bottom, at the end of your rope that the greatest revelation of Jesus' provision can come to you. Stripped bare, naked, and fully uncovered we realize: Jesus is all that we have. In that moment, everything changes— when you surrender to the grace of His perfect sufficiency.

We get so insulated and comforted by lesser things; yet the only thing we have is Jesus. In fact, He is all that we need. He is our source, the way, the truth, and the life. He is everything. He is salvation. He is healing. He is joy. He is love. He is my existence; my all and all. He makes me a good husband, father, pastor, friend—without Him I have nothing. All that I am is not enough. We, as His people, need to awaken to the reality that it is Him and Him alone who fulfills and sustains. It is only Jesus (period).

FOLLOWING JESUS

Leadership must look different in the church than in the world. You can adopt universal leadership principles, apply them to ministry, and influence masses of people. You can apply techniques and proven strategies and begin measuring impact based upon these principles. At first glance, this approach to leadership is effective, measurable, and celebrated. I would not argue that we should stop doing this altogether, but I would argue that this style of leadership is limited.

Here is the problem: God's definition of leadership stands in contrast to the world's definition. Jesus, the King of kings and our model for leadership, was betrayed, rejected, and murdered by those He led. He washed the feet of His betrayer, knowing that His crucifixion was just around the corner.

What makes a Kingdom leader different from a worldly leader? While some principles are universal, a leader in the Kingdom is very different from a leader in the world. A leader in the Kingdom must first and foremost not identify himself as a leader. A leader in the Kingdom must first and foremost identify as a follower. This is the benchmark for a Kingdom leader: one who first knows how to follow THE King.

Daily following Jesus is far different than following principles and techniques universally applied. Following Him positions us to be leaders for the one we are following. Jesus is actively leading today. And we are best positioned to lead when we are continuously following Him. When you met the Lord, you surrendered everything to Him. You laid your life, your gifts, your future, and your destiny before Him and yielded to Him as Lord and King.

> A LEADER IN THE KINGDOM MUST FIRST AND FOREMOST NOT IDENTIFY HIMSELF AS A LEADER.

Today, Jesus is looking for leaders who will re-ante their lives, their influence, and their current position before Him. We need leaders, like David, who will place the presence of God before all things. We have become too dependent on ways that seem right. We adopt what once worked for us, or what is working for someone else, and we are satisfied with doing things for Him.

The Lord told me, "There are many leaders who are influential for me, yet they are not intimate with me. I am raising up those that won't sacrifice intimacy with me for influence." These followers of Jesus will create space and opportunity for God to be God. Beyond giftings and growth strategies, He is raising up a new breed of leaders who are marked by the presence of His leadership. We must return to actively and intentionally following Him.

GIDEON

Gideon was a man who would not take the Lord's place of leadership. The people saw how God was using Gideon and his family. They came to him with a bottle of oil, and they were prepared to anoint him and his sons as their king. I pray Gideon's response would be echoed throughout pulpits and pastorates today, when he said, "I will not rule over you, nor shall my son rule over you; the Lord shall rule over you" (Judges 8:23).

The new breed of Kingdom leaders, who are following the Lord's leadership, will not receive the oil that is reserved for the Lord. They will teach and model to others that Jesus is the head of His body. Jesus, by His presence, will mark communities whose leaders will painstakingly not step into the place of influence even when God's bride wants to anoint them instead of Him.

This leadership will be costly. It is a learned and practiced humility that is culti-vated over time. It will reveal to others what

> THE LORD TOLD ME, "THERE ARE MANY LEADERS WHO ARE INFLUENTIAL FOR ME, YET THEY ARE NOT INTIMATE WITH ME. I AM RAISING UP THOSE THAT WON'T SACRIFICE INTIMACY WITH ME FOR INFLUENCE."

following the Lord looks like. It is moving with Him in the moment and listening to what He is saying. It is modeling the leadership of the Lord in moments where we would traditionally employ leadership principles common in today's church. But He does not desire to be confined to our principles. He is drawn to hunger, need, humility, and surrender. He desires to take His rightful place as Lord and King of His body.

The manifest presence of Jesus will be the fruit of surrendered leadership. And His leadership manifesting by His Spirit should be the goal of our gathering—the very intention of church leaders. In Acts 2, it was the outpouring of the Holy Spirit that led the first church meeting. Three thousand people were saved as the Holy Spirit birthed the church. His Spirit manifested as Lord; those submitted and surrendered yielded their lives (time, gifts, reputations) to His leadership. That day marked the conception of the church. God's leadership, by His Spirit, empowered anointed men and women to rightly respond to Him. This is the key for the hour ahead: the leadership of the Holy Spirit as the sustaining source of His church.

IN AND OUT

I first heard Pastor Robert Morris from Gateway Church teach on the "in and out" leadership principle. I was twenty-three and a young, green, aspiring church leader. If I'm honest, I wanted to be just like Pastor Robert. He was pastor of an emerging church in Southlake, a suburb of Dallas. It was the early days of Gateway and the early days of my own journey into ministry. I was a new and struggling youth pastor, trying to understand my calling and purpose.

Over twenty years later, I can still remember it, although I only heard the sermon once. As he spoke about the "in and out" principle, my heart began to burn. It was so simple and so clear. I knew if I could learn and apply this one activity, I would fulfill God's purpose and plan for my life. In his message, Pastor Robert outlined how learning to come in and go out was a critical benchmark for leadership throughout the Old Testament. I have continued to study this idea of coming in and going out and its relevance for leadership for a few decades now.

Let's explore in greater detail. In 2 Kings, Solomon has an encounter with the Lord that most are familiar with. In the night, God appears to Solomon and asks him the question of all questions. He tells Solomon to ask whatever he wishes, and God will grant it to him. Most everyone can tell you what Solomon asks to be granted to him—he desired wisdom. Of all things he could ask for—long life, riches, victory from enemies, or influence—Solomon asks for wisdom, and we see God is extremely pleased with his request.

This part of the story is familiar to most. Yet, what I did not realize is why Solomon had asked for wisdom. We need to see the problem facing Solomon in order to fully comprehend why this was his utmost request. Solomon was intimidated by the task at hand. His father, who preceded him, had found great favor with God, the people of Israel, and surrounding nations. Israel was flourishing, and it was up to Solomon to continue his father's legacy. Solomon knew there was one crucial element necessary for him to be able to fill his father's shoes.

In 1 Kings 3:7 we learn why Solomon chose to ask for wisdom: "And now, Lord my God, you have made Your servant king in place of my father David, yet I am like a little boy; I do not know how to go out or come in." When I heard about Solomon's plight, I could totally relate. At twenty-three years old, I knew I was young, and I had more questions than I did answers. I had never heard of this activity "coming in and going out" until it was presented in this text that Pastor Robert was teaching on.

Later that evening, after listening to the sermon, I decided that I was going to fully give myself over to understanding what Solomon meant by going out and coming in. This journey marked the next two decades of my life. And I am still in pursuit of fully understanding and practicing this concept. I am convinced it is critical for all believers, and especially church leaders today.

Turns out that "coming in and going out" is a familiar phrase in Hebrew. It is not just found in the life of Solomon—it is actually found in the life of every great leader in the Old Testament. It is a Hebraic warfare term and was an understood responsibility of Israel's leaders to execute and fulfill throughout biblical history.

Moses retired using this phrase. In Deuteronomy 31:2 he told the people of Israel, "I am a hundred and twenty years old today; I am no longer able to go out and come in." In Numbers 27, Moses prayed to the Lord about his successor. He had one request from the Lord for this leader: "May the LORD, the God of the spirits of humanity, appoint a man over the congregation, who will go out and come in before them, and lead them out and bring them in, so that the congregation of the LORD will not be like sheep that have no shepherd" (Num. 27:16-17). His one requirement was that this next leader could come in and go out; it would be the only chance of success in Moses' absence.

We find insight to this term in the life of Caleb. Caleb was Joshua's right-hand man. He was crucial to Joshua's success as the shepherd and leader of Israel. In Joshua 14, Caleb came to Joshua to request the opportunity to claim his personal inheritance. For years, Caleb had fought for everyone else's promised land, while there remained an outstanding promise for him—Moses had told Caleb that he and his relatives could live in the high country of Hebron. When Caleb approached Joshua, making the case as to why he should be permitted to claim his inheritance, he said, "Here I am this day, eighty-five years old. As yet I am as strong this day as on the day that Moses sent me; just as my strength was then, so now is my strength for war, both for going out and for coming in" (Joshua 14:10-11).

As a warfare term, Caleb explicitly said he could still fight for the promises of God by coming in and going out. This practice was an essential component for a leader to successfully lay hold of God's promises for His people.

In the first chapter of Numbers, God instructs Moses to bring forth all the fighting men of Israel, from twenty years old and upwards, to be set apart for warfare. It was the societal order for the people of Israel upon their exodus from Egypt. Imagine, for a moment, that you are a young male Israelite. You would be enlisted into the Israelite army at the age of twenty. Warfare is all-consuming. From the time you wake up to the time you fall asleep, you are keenly aware of being a soldier in the Israelite army. You are trained in bow and arrow, swordsmanship, and hand-to-hand combat.

Now, also imagine how frail and small the Israelite army was compared to the many armies they faced. Any battlefield that they marched upon; Israel was the underdog. God was choosing the weakest, smallest group of people to advance upon the enemy nations of their day. The warfare that God always had Israel engaging in was often unconventional. The strategy for Jericho was to march around walls, blow trumpets, and yell. The strategy for the Amalekites was to send Judah (worshippers) to the battlefield first. Gideon was asked to whittle his army down from 32,000 to 300 men. The list goes on and on. God was looking for people who would first come into the place of surrender and encounter (coming in) in order to go forth from that place to witness the God of Israel defeating their enemies (going out). The glory would be undoubtedly His, and the enemy troops would know that the God of Israel was the one true and living God.

A leader's ability to lead soldiers into God's presence would position them to rightly go out and wage war. An army that came to worship would be positioned to go out to witness God fight for them. It was not a matter of military tact or strength; it was about faith and trust in who was truly leading them. As the psalmist says, "Some trust in chariots and some in horses, but we trust in the Name of our God." David penned that in Psalm 20, and no one knew that better than David. From the sheep fields where he defeated lions and bears to defeating Goliath, David knew victory was only found by properly coming in and going out.

> A LEADER'S ABILITY TO LEAD SOLDIERS INTO GOD'S PRESENCE WOULD POSITION THEM TO RIGHTLY GO OUT AND WAGE WAR.

It is said that when approaching a battlefield, the army of God would erect banners over the army declaring the name of God. These banners would exalt His name on any given battlefield, in the face of any threat. The name of the Lord was key to victory. It was from the "in" that the people were positioned to see, encounter, and remember who God is, which in turn would build faith and spur confidence as they went "out" to battle.

Though we do not wage warfare like the Israelites did, we are still in a war. We must still direct God's people to go into the presence of God and out to wage war. Just like the elder in Revelation 5 directed John to behold Jesus, we must lead people into the place of worship and His presence so that

His people are bolstered in faith when they look to Jesus and are equipped to "go out" and impact whatever sphere of influence the Lord has given them. Whether it be a teacher, a businessperson, a mom, a lawyer, a pastor—you name it—we all need to regularly behold the person of Jesus and remember who our victory is. Without setting the Lord always before us (as David said), the trials, pain, and challenges we face will be too much. Life can be too hard, big, painful, or impossible. But He is the God of the impossible.

A true servant leader will give all his or her energy to leading people to see Jesus rightly—not just once during an altar call, but as a regular lifestyle. If we are not vigilant to exalt the name of the Lord and direct others to behold Him, we will instead lead people to look at our great talent, teaching, music, programs, or principles. And as wonderful as these may be, they simply do not sustain. Any twelve-step program or seven principles for successful living will not provide true food and true drink. He alone is the bread of life. We must humbly lead His people to feast on Him! We must step down from the pedestal, away from the spotlight, and out of the hot seat of everyone expecting us to have every solution. We must insist on enthroning the only one worthy.

FULLY FURNISHED

> The flesh gives birth to flesh, but the Spirit
> gives birth to the spirit.
>
> —JESUS (John 3:6)

These words are still true today. The Holy Spirit sources all that we need. If we have the Holy Spirit, we have everything that we need. The Holy Spirit is not in need of our ability to create or sustain. The Holy

Spirit will give birth to, and the grace to traverse, the journey into the fullness of God's will for our lives. Our ability to acknowledge what it is He births is crucial to continually relying on His sustenance.

What we give birth to, we are responsible for (right, parents?). What He gives birth to, He is responsible for. Many of the activities we do in church would probably continue if the Holy Spirit were not present—activities that I believe God has honored, but that He did not instigate.

There is a growing trend around leadership and influencing people. The wisdom of these principles centers upon our ability to reach and impact people. These wisdom principles could not only be applied to the church, but any organization that is in the business of impact.

Take a platform like social media. We can learn the tricks of the trade and grow quite the following. We might use that platform to attract thousands or possibly millions to our message. This is a great way to reach people for the gospel if God has birthed it. So, this begs the question: how do I know what God is birthing?

Your history with God is important. Growing up, I did not know that I could have a personal history with God. Yet, over time and seasons, God guides, directs, and confirms. He will lead us into places and opportunities that we could not possibly get to in our own strength.

One of Jesus's descriptions of the upper room in Mark 14 is that the disciples would find a "fully furnished" upper room. Jesus was telling His disciples that they would find exactly what they needed when they arrived at the upper room to prepare Passover. Basically, He was saying, "If you don't have it, you don't need it."

I believe what was true in the natural for the disciples back then is true for us in a spiritual sense today. The good news of the gospel comes fully furnished—for individual lives and collective communities of faith.

We have everything that we need to accomplish all that we are called to do. If we are born again, you and I lack nothing. He is the supplier of needs—perfect provision.

The fully furnished description did not mean a lot to me in the early days of the upper room. Initially, I was pretty confident in what I could do and what I brought to the equation. The season of stripping I described in chapter one was the greatest gift God could have given me.

After the Lord stripped me of me, I actually got comfortable approaching church unconventionally. From the early and empty prayer room meetings to our extended times of worship during our services, to having a bench of incredible teachers regularly on schedule, we were convicted of our one corporate aim: we gathered for Him. We found success in His arrival and Him being ministered to. For many years, the meetings were small, but Jesus liked coming, and that was all that mattered to us.

With that focus, the core team I was leading grew accustomed to me saying He is all that we need. If He comes, we are successful. His presence is the goal. His presence is the win. If He shows up, we have accomplished our goal in gathering. Whether it is a prayer meeting or a weekly service, a small group or staff meeting, His presence is always the point. What I had to continually repeat as an early leader, our community now fully embraces fourteen years later.

THE GOOD NEWS OF THE GOSPEL COMES FULLY FURNISHED—FOR INDIVIDUAL LIVES AND COLLECTIVE COMMUNITIES OF FAITH.

Even in the initial stages of church planting, I kept describing the UPPERROOM as fully furnished. Jesus said it about the original upper room, and we declared it about ours. If we didn't have something (i.e.

children's pastor, newcomers class, etc.), we didn't actually need it. We possessed everything needed to be successful as a community. It was the active discipline to tend to Jesus first and foremost that resulted in more people, more fruit, more testimonies, and of course...more fun.

If someone suggested a need for something we did not have, we would look around to see if there was an answer to the need. If there was not a person or resource already within our church family, we concluded that it was not a need the Lord was addressing. He had not yet provided it, so we did not yet need it. Again, the preeminent need we had as a community was His coming and His leadership.

This lesson was invaluable to me, because as a leader in the natural, I was trained to problem solve and meet needs--from family to kids to singles to everyone else. As the pastor, my focus was to ensure we were meeting the needs of people. Yet, I quickly learned the UPPERROOM was not about me or us as a church meeting the needs of people. The UPPERROOM was about positioning people to behold Jesus and have their needs met by Him.

> UPPERROOM WAS ABOUT POSITIONING PEOPLE TO BEHOLD JESUS AND HAVE THEIR NEEDS MET BY HIM.

He is sufficient and more than able to meet people in their need. In fact, He is much better at doing it than you or I ever could be. From the homosexual attending church for the first time, to the wealthy, affluent businessman who was so out of place in our initial meetings, Jesus was able and willing to meet each individual exactly where they were. What people need modeled for them are leaders who are first and foremost following Jesus—leaders who are not driven by others' needs, but by looking to the One who could meet every need.

Chapter 6

KING DAVID: A CASE STUDY FOR BIBLICAL LEADERSHIP

Anyone who understands the Bible at any level knows the importance of King David's life in the overarching story of God's redemptive plan. The descriptions scripture shares about his life are second to none. He is most widely recognized as the man who was after God's own heart. It is written that he fulfilled every purpose that God had for him in his generation. He is known for his ability to slay giants, conquer kingdoms, and to soothe souls and cause demons to flee through his harp playing. He was a poet and a prophet. He was a conquering king and a humble servant. David's life was said to be rooted by Jesus Christ Himself. In fact, Jesus will eternally sit upon the throne of David. His leadership is unparalleled in all of Israel's history.

Many have written about what made David such an example of a leader and hero of faith. His life has been studied, preached about, and celebrated. Christians, Jews, and Muslims all honor his life and his legacy, and every leader in Israel after David would be measured by his life and reign as king.

Yet, what made David so unique? What brought such immense favor to his life and established his legacy that we now know of and honor? I believe the answer is found in one verse.

BRINGING BACK THE ARK

This specific verse is in First Chronicles 13. At this point in David's life, he is around the age of thirty-seven. He had likely already been anointed as the future leader of Israel for over twenty years. He had waited in the back-forty of the sheep fields after his initial encounter with Samuel the prophet. He slayed Goliath and was launched into the national limelight as a hero and warrior. He had played the harp in the intimate chambers of Saul's palace, the man who eventually would become his greatest adversary. For at least a decade, he lived on the run, considered a rebel leader by his own nation who did not understand his calling nor destiny. He divided the nation when he became King of Judah because Israel had not fully accepted him. And in the thirteenth chapter of First Chronicles, everything changed.

For the first time in his life, everyone in the nation was completely unified under David as their king. At that moment, the leaders, generals, and fathers of the nation all agreed that David was God's chosen leader of Israel—the least likely person for this position, but obviously with God's favor and grace upon his life. What God had acknowledged decades earlier, the entire nation now recognized. David was king.

David gathered the nation for the first time to address them as their king. He was primed to state the political agenda of his reign and unveil to everyone why God had positioned him to lead. It was at this moment the nation would witness what God valued in His chosen leader.

In the United States, our government annually has a State of the Union address. It is a significant night when the president addresses every branch of leadership in the U.S. government. Every senator, congressman, military general, and supreme court judge is present for this evening. It is the moment where our nation's leader sets the political agenda before the nation. The primetime television networks air the speech along with every major radio outlet. All eyes and ears are on our nation's leader to hear directly from their mouth where we are going as a nation, and how the president plans to get us there.

For newly anointed King David, First Chronicles 13 is his State of the Union moment. It was his first public address as their leader, and he would set his agenda as their king. David's agenda is paramount for us to hear and understand in order to comprehend why he was a man after God's heart. His statement should be studied, learned, and relearned. I believe it is the most important statement David would make in his entire life, and the very reason why he was in the position he was in. He addressed the entire assembly of Israel as follows:

"If it seems good to you, and if it is from the Lord our God, let us send word everywhere to our kinsmen who remain in all the land of Israel, and to the priests and Levites who are with them in their cities with pasture lands, that they meet with us; and let us bring back the ark of our God to us, since we did not seek it in the days of Saul" (1 Chron. 13:2-3).

I can only imagine the critics in David's day responding to his speech. Are you kidding me? You want us to focus on the BOX?! There are too many pressing issues facing us today. The Philistines, whom you befriended, are surrounding us. Our economy is struggling. We have had a civil war surrounding the former king's obsession over you, and this is your plan? It had to have been absurd to every ear listening to their newly anointed king that day.

Yet this was the plan. David's first and foremost agenda was to pursue the ark of God. His great unveiling was to seek the ark and put it at the center of the entire nation. I believe David had waited years for this moment. Moreso,

I believe God had waited years for this moment. David's one desire as the leader of that nation was to put the True Leader, once again, in His rightful place as King of Israel. The prioritization of the ark would forever mark David's reign. And the ark was the distinguishing difference between David's kingship and King Saul.

> HE KNEW THE LEADER OF HIS PEOPLE HAD TO FIRST BE A SEEKER OF HIS PRESENCE.

This statement gives us incredible insight into what made David the leader he was. This statement was not just David unveiling his national agenda as king, but I believe this statement was the revealing of why God had chosen David as king. He knew that all David had faithfully done throughout his life, he would continue to do as the leader of God's people. God knew He had first and foremost found a follower of His leadership. God anointed David's desire for His people's sake, and ultimately for His name's sake. He knew the leader of His people had to first be a seeker of His presence.

THE ARK OF THE COVENANT

The ark of the covenant represented God's manifest presence, power, and glory on the earth. Prior to the cross and giving of the Holy Spirit, the ark is where God's presence rested. He could not dwell in men as He does today. Christ had not yet come, and the once-and-for-all sacrifice had not yet been made. Therefore, God chose to dwell upon the mercy seat of the ark of the covenant.

We will look at how David fulfilled this mandate, but I want you to first see how radical his mandate was at that time. It was singular, focused, extreme, and it would be incredibly costly. David's declaration of this agenda would put any and every other agenda second to this primary agenda. The ark of God would be the nation's pursuit not only in the first couple of months of David's reign, but for the remainder of his days. David would exhaust every resource that he possibly could in order to direct the people's attention to the ark of God.

In this way, from day one, David distinguished how he was different from Saul as a leader. What we have done in the past we can no longer do. What we have neglected in the past, we can no longer neglect. My leadership will have a completely different focus than what you are used to. We will not focus on defeating our enemies, meeting our nation's needs, or any other noble pursuit; we will first and foremost pursue the ark of God.

I believe the global church is at the same crossroads today as the nation of Israel was in First Chronicles 13. God is raising up a new breed of leadership that will devote their attention, resources, and leadership back to God's manifest presence among us. It is to be our dedicated pursuit if we truly believe His presence is the answer for every pressing need of our day. His presence has been, and always will be, our surest and most powerful source.

> DAVID WOULD EXHAUST EVERY RESOURCE THAT HE POSSIBLY COULD IN ORDER TO DIRECT THE PEOPLE'S ATTENTION TO THE ARK OF GOD.

Throughout the Old Testament, we see the house of the Lord was central to the success or the failure of the nation. There are seven recorded revivals in the Old Testament and all of them were the result of a leader who reestablished God's temple and pursued the ark as their primary mandate. If a leader tended to the presence of the Lord, the nation flourished. If it was disregarded, the nation suffered and oftentimes was destroyed. A leader who was not establishing God's dwelling on earth and honoring His name was a leader who would become wayward and serve other gods. There was no middle ground. It was either one or the other.

Why is today any different? We have made things way too complicated, and with all the complexities of our day come a number of questions and issues that leaders feel the need to address. Leaders get easily distracted attempting to answer the many questions and needs of those around us, while the answer is always singular and much simpler. The leadership crisis on the earth today is about the presence of the Lord being established in a dwelling place for the Lord. This may seem trite or too simplistic, but I believe it is extremely simple.

TABERNACLE OF DAVID

Did you know there was a stark difference between the tabernacle of Moses and the tabernacle of David? To be honest with you, I did not know much about David's tabernacle. As a seminary student, we never discussed David's tabernacle. If I recall all the sermons over the decades I grew up in church, I can't recall one time hearing about David's tabernacle. And if you google "tabernacle of David," you will be hard-pressed to find any major voice in today's evangelical world talking about the significance of David's tabernacle in scripture, or its relevance for us today.

In contrast, most of us can offer commentary about Moses's tabernacle. We know about the outer courts, inner courts, and holiest of holies. We can recall sermon series on the various facets of Moses's tabernacle and the priestly roles associated with the sacrificial system. It is a beautiful depiction of the cross and has great implications for us as the people of God today. So, I was honestly taken aback when I first discovered how different David's tabernacle was from Moses' tabernacle.

We know that David had a desire to establish a resting place for the Lord—a place for the ark of God to reside and for His people to have access to call upon His name (1 Chron. 16:6). He desired to establish an environment where God would habitat among His people. This desire, I believe, was not just David's desire, but the Lord's. We know from the beginning of creation that God has desired to rest on earth, among His people. In David, He found a leader who desired the same thing.

In that pursuit, David discovered an order for the Lord's habitation. This order would not replace Moses's tabernacle, rather it would fulfill it. Interesting enough, during the reign of Saul, Moses's tabernacle was in full operation at Mount Gibeah. The daily activities of the priests, the sacrificial systems, and all the protocols were in full effect. Yet, during Saul's reign, the ark of the covenant did not reside within the temple's holiest of holies. It had not been transported from Kiriath-jearim, the location it was stored after its return from Philistine captivity (1 Sam. 7).

Prior to David's reign, the tabernacle of Moses had a form, structure, and regular activities, but it did not have the very substance of God's presence within the tabernacle. Isn't this an accurate depiction of religion? Practice with no power; function and form without intimacy and relationship? The presence of God had been removed from the very systems and structures that He had designed to lead us to His presence.

David knew that systems and structures were flawed because the people were neglecting the very purpose and reason they existed—God's presence among them. Under his leadership, he would reveal to the nation (and to the future church), how to rightly host God. I believe the tabernacle that David established was the single most extravagant place of worship the world has ever seen since the creation in Genesis to the present.

For thirty-three years, David's tabernacle continually hosted worship and praise. From the resources David expended, to the prophetic literature that would be written, nothing compares to the organization of continual day and night devotion to the Lord.

So, what was it that David actually built?

For thirty-three years, David assigned thousands of Levites to worship in an open room around the ark of the covenant. In his tabernacle, there would be no blood offerings to the Lord, only the offerings of praise and thanksgiving. In an open room with no separate rooms or dividing veils, David gave the nations access to the ark of God, and, therefore, the presence of God on earth.

David employed over 8,000 fulltime singers, musicians, and gate-keepers to tend to the ark. In modern day numbers, he would spend a few billion dollars every year to finance this endeavor. He established a worship order that was inspired by the Holy Spirit and is a prophetic picture of what is happening right now in heaven.

According to Revelation chapters 4 and 5, God the Father and God the Son sit enthroned in heaven surrounded by prayer, music, and song. Elders regularly bow down in worship, play harps, and hold golden bowls of incense, which are our prayers—the prayers of the saints. The twenty-four elders and the four living creatures are constantly giving thanks and singing a new song. Myriads of angels join in the chorus; it never stops, day or night. David must have caught a prophetic glimpse of this heavenly reality by the manner in which he designed the tabernacle.

In David's tabernacle, roughly two thirds of Psalms were written—the modern-day worship songs that continue to be sung to this day. The scribes of David's day would pen the prophetic utterances of the minstrels and psalmists. Words like "better is one day in your courts, than a thousand elsewhere" would be written. Day and night, night and day, unceasing, perpetual, unending worship and devotion to the Lord took place.

It was as if God allowed David to build a structure that superseded his day and current covenant. No one would have ever dreamed of doing what David did. He was a radical and prophetic lover and pursuer of God. And lovers and pursuers of God discover a grace to unlock in their generation a heavenly outpouring reserved for the ages to come. David tapped into the very relationship that we, now under the new covenant, experience and have with the Lord. No longer would there be need for blood offerings and animal sacrifices because Jesus' one sacrifice would be a sufficient offering for all time.

David provided a preview for the world to see what God's eternal tabernacle would be. God's resting place on earth was unveiled through the leadership of this man after His own heart. David built a house of prayer for all nations that established God's Kingdom on earth and in Israel. This revelation is mind blowing for us to understand, and its ramifications are significant for faith leaders today.

ACTS AND AMOS

David's tabernacle also shows up in the New Testament at the first Christian "conference" ever held by early church leaders, recorded in Acts 15. At that time, the church was experiencing great strain because of the number of Gentiles coming to The Way as believers in Jesus the Messiah. The Jewish leadership of the church was grappling with the Gentiles' impact on the church. Once outsiders, they were now to be considered and accepted as family, and there was a growing sense of concern among the Jewish church leaders. Doctrinal stances on circumcision, food, and drink were causing division among the various branches of the early church. That division was crucial to address for the sake of the gospel advancement.

Various brethren were teaching salvation through circumcision. It was a "Jesus and _____" message. They were preaching Jesus and additional works for salvation. As we know, Jesus "and" anything is a zero for the gospel. The one who is everything, the all in all, cannot be "part" of something. He is all and everything, so there is no "Jesus and"; the gospel is Jesus only.

Any additional works would devalue the complete and finished work of the cross, and it was at that leadership summit in Acts 15 that the Apostles addressed this grievous error. In Acts 15:7, Luke recorded three specific revelations from the leadership summit that came "after there had been much debate."

I think it is funny he included that detail. If you have ever been part of a good religious discussion, elder meeting, or church staff meeting, you know how well we Christians can "debate." I can only imagine what that one line probably entailed. "After there had been much debate" could have been hours, days, or even weeks of discussions. We don't know; yet we do know what the three most important resolutions were after the debate.

First, we have Peter's exhortation. He states that no other yoke should be placed upon the Gentiles. "We believe that we are saved through the grace of the Lord Jesus, in the same way as they also are" (Acts 15:11). This is the good news of the gospel. We are all saved through the same act of the man Jesus, and our faith in His death and resurrection results in salvation. It is the transforming power of God's grace at work in our lives, attainable by faith for all humankind. Regardless of your nationality, race, economic status, God's grace is available to all through the saving grace of His Son's work. This is crucial for us to see and understand. This recording in Acts 15 represents the PROCLAMATION of the gospel.

The next recorded conversation was through the mouths of Paul and Barnabas. In verse 12, it says that "All the people kept silent, and they were listening to Barnabas and Paul as they were relating all the signs and wonders that God had done through them among the Gentiles." After Peter offered the proclamation of the gospel, the Bible records the DEMONSTRATION of the gospel to the Gentiles. It was not just the words of the gospel, but the manifestation of the gospel in power—signs, wonders, and the filling of the Holy Spirit.

It is imperative that a demonstration of the gospel accompany every proclamation of the gospel. We should expect a demonstration of the power of the gospel to coincide with every gospel proclamation. This is the "word and deed" of the gospel (Rom. 15:18-19). Paul described this as fully preaching the gospel to the Gentiles.

I indicated this chapter is about the tabernacle of David, so you might be wondering why I am unpacking a seemingly random church conference in Acts 15. Yet, the Holy Spirit highlighted one more participant's commentary from the deliberations at the council in Jerusalem. This time it would be the words of James, the brother of Jesus.

After Peter, Paul, and Barnabas, James shares an Old Testament prophecy to prove that the Gentiles were to be taken as a people for His name (15:14). He then quotes an obscure prophecy from the prophet Amos:

"On that day I will raise up the tabernacle of David, which has fallen down, and repair its damages; I will raise up its ruins, and rebuild it as in the days of old; that they may possess the remnant of Edom, and all the Gentiles who are called by My name," says the Lord who does this thing.

—Amos 9:11-12, NKJV

This is profound. Out of all the Old Testament prophecies James could have quoted, he chose this one mentioning David's tabernacle. Now, I know the primary context is the Gentile nations coming into the faith and accessing salvation. Certainly, this is a primary takeaway from James' commentary. I agree completely with this interpretation and application. David's tabernacle was accessible to Gentiles and this reference to Amos' prophecy and the Gentiles' access to the Lord is a way in which His tabernacle would be restored and rebuilt. This text is also an invitation for all to understand what the restoration of His tabernacle means for us today. This restoration is unto the CELEBRATION of what we all have received by His grace.

> WE ARE ALL INVITED TO PROCLAIM SALVATION, DEMONSTRATE SALVATION, AND TO CELEBRATE SALVATION.

These three revelations by the Holy Spirit are imperative for us to acknowledge and apply. Peter highlights the proclamation of the gospel. Paul and Barnabas relay the demonstration of the gospel. James highlights the celebration of the gospel. This revelation, and re-establishment of David's tabernacle is an invitation for all people to experience the accessible presence of God. We are all invited to proclaim salvation, demonstrate salvation, and to celebrate salvation.

IMPLICATIONS OF DAVID'S TABERNACLE FOR THE MODERN CHURCH

David's tabernacle is a model for how all believers are to rightly respond to the gospel today. Once we have heard the proclamation and seen the powerful demonstration of the gospel, we must rightly respond by celebrating the gospel.

In the tabernacle of David, this celebration was established with perpetual praise, thanksgiving, prayer, and worship unto the Lord. Now we, as living tabernacles, are to live lives of perpetual praise and thanksgiving based on what God has accomplished for us as His people.

> Rejoice always, pray without ceasing, in everything give thanks; for this is the will of God in Christ Jesus for you.
> —1 Thes. 5:16-18, NKJV

Corporately, we who were once far off, have now been brought near through the blood of His Son (Eph. 2:13). The only right response is to establish a people of praise on the earth, eternally grateful for what we have received through His loving, sacrificial, and perfect act of redemption.

David's tabernacle is a prototype of the worshiping church and an invitation for all today to establish a resting place for the Lord on the earth. Through praise and thanksgiving, worship, and intercession, we create resting places on the earth today for God's presence to reveal to us His nearness, nature, and power.

Long before the words of Jesus, David tapped into God's desire for His house to be a house of prayer, accessible to all people, because of the one and complete sacrifice of the perfect Lamb. As referenced earlier, seven revivals occurred in the Old Testament under the righteous kings, David being the first one. There is one common denominator in every revival: a leader got revelation of the Davidic order of worship and implemented the Levitical call to minister to the Lord through continual worship.

That is why Jesus had the right to rebuke the religious leadership in His day and call them to repentance. He knew they had a recorded history in the scriptures where they could have discerned what a "house of prayer" looked like—it would have looked like the tabernacle of David.

PSALM 132: THE COST

God is raising up leaders who have a singular focus. The outpouring of God's Spirit will not come through happenstance or chance. Leaders, like David, will settle for nothing less than His presence. As we respond to the Lord's invitation to lead with this singular pursuit, it is important to acknowledge the costliness of this pursuit.

David paid a high price to create a resting place for God. We learn about the strength and nature of David's resolve in Psalm 132. Psalm 132 is one of the most important psalms penned about the life of David. Most attribute the authorship of Psalm 132 to Solomon, David's son. Whomever it was, he was reflecting on a vow that David had made with the Lord.

> Remember, O LORD, on David's behalf, all his affliction;
> How he swore to the LORD and vowed to the Mighty One
> of Jacob, "Surely I will not enter my house, nor lie on my bed;
> I will not give sleep to my eyes or slumber to my eyelids, until
> I find a place for the LORD, a dwelling place for the Mighty
> One of Jacob."
>
> —Psalm 132:1-5

This vow was the driving force of David's life. It consumed his every waking hour. He desired to establish a place where all could enter this dwelling place to worship. It would be a place where the Lord would enter and abide.

In return, the psalmist says that the Lord responded and made a vow to David. In essence the Lord said, "Because you have made this vow with me, I, in return, will make a vow to you." This vow is found in Psalm 132:11. The Lord promised to establish David's descendants and abundantly bless him with provision—food, clothes, protection, and salvation would be found because of his pursuit.

This one thing would impact everything. This one thing would be the greatest thing David would accomplish. It would also cost David everything. In fact, Psalm 132 begins with a remembrance of all of David's afflictions precisely because of the vow he had made. His vow was forged in the place of anonymity and persecution—he was misunderstood and in exile. But I believe this vow and singular pursuit is what established David as a man after God's own heart.

> THERE IS ONE COMMON DENOMINATOR IN EVERY REVIVAL: A LEADER GOT REVELATION OF THE DAVIDIC ORDER OF WORSHIP AND IMPLEMENTED THE LEVITICAL CALL TO MINISTER TO THE LORD THROUGH CONTINUAL WORSHIP.

David did eventually fulfill his vow to the Lord, but after a major learning curve. David attempted to bring the ark from Kiriath-jearim to Jerusalem. It was only an eight-mile journey, but within those eight miles, David learned the price it took to carry the ark. Approaching the presence of God was no trivial matter. In 1 Chronicles 13, the exciting pronouncement to bring the ark back is followed by a tragic event—the death of Uzzah. The ark must be pursued according to the prescribed biblical measures.

You see, David devised his own strategy for carrying the ark, neglecting to inquire of the Lord first. He set two men, Ahio and Uzzah, near the ark to accompany it back to Jerusalem. David used a new structure, consisting of boards pulled by oxen, to transport the ark. Ahio means "brotherly" and Uzzah's name means "strength." These two men were brave and had an extraordinary responsibility. I can only imagine the task at hand and how they must have felt to be so close to the ark. David's strategy was to surround the ark with two men whose names collectively mean the brother's strength. This strategy proved to be tragic for the two nearest the ark and would result in Uzzah (strength) being killed.

This was not Uzzah's fault. Uzzah's death was the result of David's poor decision. His death was the result of David's strategy in carrying the ark. This not only resulted in Uzzah's death but also brought reproach on a national level to David and his agenda. "This is what happens when the box comes out into the public. People die."

David became angry because of this outcome, and he became terrified of God (1 Chron. 13:10-11). This would prove to be a profound moment, not only for Israel, but for everyone who desired to be near to the Lord. God was not impressed with David's strategy, and David realized his strength and gifts were not sufficient in effectively seeking the ark.

This story has significant implications for us today as we attempt to pursue God's presence. Those two men, Ahio and Uzzah, represented the best that Israel had to offer. They represented men's strengths and gifts. But God had not asked to be surrounded by their strengths; He desired to be in relationship with them according to His ordained order. God would come to His people on His terms and not theirs.

David, fearful, embarrassed, and at a loss, resorted to putting the ark away once again. He stowed it in Obed-Edom's home and did some deep soul-searching. He must have opened the Torah with one burning question: "What am I doing wrong? How am I to rightly seek you as the anointed leader of Israel?" We don't know how David discovered what he did, but we do know the outcome. It is two chapters later in 1 Chronicles 15.

In 1 Chronicles 15:13, David realized that he and the people did not pursue God according to God's prescribed measures. David had assumed his passionate desire to seek God was sufficient. If he sought the ark and did it in excellence (or strength), God would honor this desire and this pursuit. After all, David's heart as a leader was to follow and honor the Lord. He was placing the long-neglected ark of God's presence before the people.

Desire, excellence, and strength are not enough. There was an ancient and prescribed means that God had ordained to rightly approach Him. David's discovery has eternal ramifications for us as God's people—he discovered the significance of the Levite.

David makes a bold announcement in 1 Chronicles 15:1-2. He erected a tent named David's tent and declared that "No one except the Levites are to carry the ark of God. The Lord has chosen them to carry the ark of God and to minister to Him forever."

God still has specific desires and ways to approach Him. As new covenant believers, we would not concern ourselves with tracking down those with the Levitical bloodline to "carry the ark" of His presence. However, the spirit of the Levitical heart to minister to the Lord is absolutely relevant today. The Levitical order represents God's desire to be surrounded with worship—music and song, thanksgiving, and praise. It is what David learned and it is what is currently happening around His throne in heaven (Rev. 4 and 5).

Today, a worship movement is emerging that will far exceed David's. There are thousands of young "Davids" right now whom God has made a similar covenant with. These leaders are gripped by God's purposes and marked by His presence. This group of leaders will usher in the second coming of Jesus. The Lord is orchestrating a people who will be ready for His return. These communities will be marked with similar qualities and expressions as David's tabernacle. In these communities, our spiritual appetite will be ruined for anything but God's presence alone. Business as usual will not satisfy. Sunday morning Christianity won't suffice. Modern day Levites will count the cost and gladly lay down their lives to establish resting places for God's presence all over the earth.

> DESIRE, EXCELLENCE, AND STRENGTH ARE NOT ENOUGH. THERE WAS AN ANCIENT AND PRESCRIBED MEANS THAT GOD HAD ORDAINED TO RIGHTLY APPROACH HIM.

CREATION AND COVENANT

David learned and lived in covenant with God. The vow he made with God in Psalm 132 was the reason he built what he built. David's tabernacle was the fruit of his covenant with God. And the tabernacle he built released a creative expression of songs, sounds, and writings that are still marking the earth today.

Covenant results in creativity expressed and further cultivated. When people are grounded in a covenant, the natural overflow of that covenant will be creativity. In the coming days, as we become established in God's gospel covenant of grace, the church is going to lead in the creative expression of art, songs, film, video, and design.

Creative expressions are crucial for the proclamation of the gospel in the days ahead. Musicians, artists, and poets will lead the charge in the coming days. For too long, the church has been relegated to two to three songs and a sermon. While creativity can be expressed through these gifts, there is so much more for us than the limitation of one to two hours on a weekend, or a small handful of people demonstrating the Lord's creativity through them.

We must awaken everyone to the inclusive and adventurous invitation to express the gospel through creativity from covenant. Covenant was always intended to be expressed. Freedom is the fruit of covenant, and the truest expressions of that freedom are people expressing their new natures (creations) in their assigned context.

You and I are created in the image of the Creator. In our God-given design and constructs, each of us were created to express Him to the world. Through our giftings and callings, we are designed to release to the world who now lives within us.

THREE COVENANTS

Theologically, there are three primary covenants God has established. He has two covenants with mankind and one covenant with Himself. With mankind, God first established the covenant of works. This covenant was based upon an established agreement He made with man.

In the beginning, Adam was under the covenant of works. His one duty that He agreed to fulfill was to not eat from the one tree in the garden. If Adam would not eat from the tree, God would provide everything he could need. God would dwell with Adam, and Adam with God, based upon this one statute. We know how that turned out. Adam and Eve transgressed, yet God, in His mercy, continued to pursue them.

The covenant of works evolved over time, as we see in the covenant of the law with Moses and the Israelites. The ten commandments eventually grew into more than 600 commandments. The understanding was that if you abide by these commands, your covenant (or right standing) with God would remain intact.

This covenant of works was obviously limited. We could never fulfill our end of the bargain, so God established another covenant with humankind. This covenant is the covenant of grace. The parties to this covenant of grace are God and the people He redeems. But in this case, Christ fills the special role as "mediator," in which He fulfills the conditions of the covenant for us, thereby reconciling us to God.

There was no mediator between God and man in the covenant of works. This is the beautiful news of the gospel. What we could not do for ourselves (under the covenant of works), God does for us through the grace of His Son. As a perfect man, He fulfilled the covenant of works so that by our faith in His work, we could be redeemed.

You may be thinking, "thanks for the theology course of covenants... what's your point?" Understanding the significance of God's two covenants with humankind leads us to the greatest covenant ever made. It is called the covenant of redemption. Before anything ever existed, God made a covenant with Himself. Before the foundations of the earth, God established a redemptive plan that He would execute through Himself. This is the covenant of redemption.

God, the Father, was in covenant with God, the Son, and with God, the Spirit. Before anything came into existence, God the Father agreed to send His one and only Son to earth to reveal Himself and be a powerful and perfect offering for us. At that time, God, the Son, Jesus Christ agreed to fully become a man in the flesh. He agreed to be our representative, obey the demands of the covenant of works on our behalf, and pay the penalty for sin, which we deserved (John 17:2-6 John 3:16, Romans 5:18-19; Col 2:9; Heb 9:24, 10:5). The Holy Spirit agreed to fill the Son and empower Him to carry out His ministry (Matthew 3:16; Luke 4:1,14,18 John 3:34) and to apply the benefits of Christ's redemptive work to believers (John 14:16-17,26 Acts 1:8; 2:17-18,33). This was all agreed upon before any plan of creation was put in place.

God, in covenant with God, the Trinity, gave them the freedom to create. The created order rested upon this foundation that God had a plan from beginning to end. This is a fascinating revelation for us. When God said, "Let there be light," He was speaking from the place of covenant with Himself. Creation was God's expression of the covenant that He had made with Himself. Creativity is the byproduct of covenant.

This truth is found throughout scripture. The next time we see it is in the story of Noah. We are familiar with the story. God is grieved He created man. His spirit was contending against all of humankind, and He sent the floods, destroying all people on earth. Yet, He already had a plan of redemption. He found Noah, a righteous man, to build an ark. Noah and his relatives were spared from the flood. For forty days, Noah and his family were hidden in the ark while God purified the earth. When Noah emerged from the ark, God immediately made a covenant again with man through Noah. His promise was to never flood the earth again. It was a secondary covenant that is still in effect today. God will never destroy the earth with a flood.

> CREATIVITY IS THE BYPRODUCT OF COVENANT.

Upon making this agreement with Noah, what does God do? He expresses that covenant through a symbol that we still see today. A creative expression called a rainbow. I am not sure a rainbow had ever been seen prior to this moment in time. Yet, God, recently establishing a covenant with Noah, creates a new expression of beauty in the skies, pointing all people for all time to this covenant.

In Exodus 35, we see this truth demonstrated again when God formalized His covenant with Moses and the terms of the covenant with all the people of Israel. Everyone understood and agreed to the terms and there was great excitement among the Israelites. So, what did God do? He filled one man with the Holy Spirit in the nation of Israel. In fact, this is the first mention of a person being filled with the Holy Spirit we see in the Old Testament. God filled a man named Bezalel with the Holy Spirit. This infilling came for a specific purpose and reason. He was filled to express the newly established covenant through creativity. It says in Exodus 35:30-35:

> Moses said to the sons of Israel, "See, the Lord has called by name Bezalel.... And He has filled him with the Spirit of God, in wisdom, in understanding, in knowledge, and in all craftsmanship; to create designs for working in gold, in silver, and in bronze, and in the cutting of stones for settings and in the carving of wood, so as to perform in every inventive work. He also has put in his heart to teach, both he and Oholiab, the son of Ahisamach, of the tribe of Dan. He has filled them with skill to perform every work of an engraver, of a designer, and of an embroiderer, in violet, purple, and in scarlet material, and in fine linen, and of a weaver, as performers of every work and makers of designs."

God filled Bezalel with His Spirit for creative design. The first human being ever filled with the Spirit of God was to express creativity under the infilling and influence of the Spirit. Design, craftsmanship, cutting, carving, engraving, embroidering, weaving, sewing, and every needed skill for design are mentioned. God desired to express in excellence, beauty, and brilliance the statutes of His covenant with His people.

Similarly, we see this in our natural relationships when a man and woman formalize their love in a marital covenant. Upon engagement, plans are made for a wedding ceremony. The purpose of this ceremony is to publicly make covenant with each other and the Lord.

Before family and friends, the bride and groom make vows to one another and to the Lord. They make commitments to remain together for better or worse, in sickness and health, whether rich or poor, and until death. This moment in time is a supernatural exchange when two individuals become one in the eyes of the Lord. They leave their mother and father's home and establish their own family based upon this covenant. This marital covenant is older than sin itself. It survived the fall of the garden and is a gift given to us by God. Marriage remains God's righteous plan for a family to be in covenant with each other and with Him.

> THE FIRST HUMAN BEING EVER FILLED WITH THE SPIRIT OF GOD WAS TO EXPRESS CREATIVITY UNDER THE INFILLING AND INFLUENCE OF THE SPIRIT.

From the wedding ceremony, the couple go to the marital bed to express their marital covenant through their sexuality. In this order, we see God's design that sex be reserved for the context and security of a marriage covenant. This expression is the most intimate act a man and woman can share. God says this act is the act where the two become one flesh in the union of body, soul, and spirit. Sex is a physical, emotional, and spiritual coming together of a husband and wife. Through this act of love, something happens. It is from this covenant that the two will procreate. The union of the two will produce an expression of their covenant. They will procreate life through their covenant of love.

Our kids are the creative expression of the covenant we have with one another through the Lord. When you see one of our four children, you physically see how Lorisa and I are "one flesh" in the way our children exhibit both of our features. When we came together in sexual intimacy, we procreated through that union, to produce a creative expression of covenant.

Like Bezalel, we enter into covenant by the power of the Holy Spirit and are born again. Again, creativity is the expression of covenant. You and I were dead before God, and by grace we are born again, filled with the Holy Spirit, and declared "a new creation." As believers, we live expressing the freedom, fruit, gifts, and life of one redeemed by God. Our lives are to be creative expressions of the covenant of grace we have with God through His son.

When the church emerges confident in covenant with God, it will produce the most creative explosion of beauty and brilliance the earth has seen. From art and design, documentaries and films, media and music, entrepreneurs and marketplaces, the church will lead the world in the most powerful creativity of God's loving nature. People rooted in the depth, height, width, and length of the love of God will be given vision and provision for expressions that will expand His Kingdom across the globe. Religion does not produce this expression, and our doctrinal beliefs alone will not produce this expression. It is through our confidence in His powerful covenant of grace, and renewal of the understanding that we are divine image-bearers, that heaven will come to earth through supernatural creativity.

Within David's tabernacle, he created an atmosphere for others to find their creative expression as God's people. The psalmist sang. The dancers danced. The scribes captured. The prophets prophesied. All of Israel experienced the blessing and favor of God in covenant with His people.

THE DEVIL HATES COVENANT

The devil seeks to steal, kill, and destroy covenant. He knows the power of a person or people established in the freedom that only covenant can bring. From sexuality to the arts, the enemy has attempted to redefine biblical freedom and covenant. There are various examples but none clearer than the homosexual agenda sweeping the earth today.

For years he has desensitized us to sexual immorality, especially homosexuality. It has gone from being illegal, to a social taboo, to now being completely accepted, defended, and celebrated. This sexual expression has ultimately led to the undermining of the biblical marriage covenant between a man and a woman, and therefore disrupted the power of covenant creativity available to us. Clearly, the design of God's covenant between man and woman is the only way to procreate.

People were created to be free. We were designed to live and experience freedom. The "sexual freedom" the enemy is serving to our culture is a superficial freedom that is catalyzing sexual bondage and addiction, and an independence from God's design and perfect order. It is humanistic in focus and will not lead to the true freedom that is only found in surrendered intimacy with Jesus. Only Jesus can provide true freedom, joy, and satisfaction in your sexuality. The beauty and creativity of your sexuality was designed for covenant, first with Him, and forever sustained by Him. Any other sexual expression outside of God's covenant is a counterfeit of heavenly design. It is the very scheme of the enemy—to offer us a false freedom and counterfeit intimacy.

CELEBRATION OF THE GOSPEL TODAY

I am convinced the same Spirit that spurred David to build God a temple is the same Spirit within us, still desiring to establish a resting place for God today. I am not suggesting that we tailor our churches after David's tent exactly, but God still desires resting places on the earth where His people minister to Him perpetually through thanksgiving, praise, and worship.

> IT IS THROUGH THE RIGHT RESPONSE AND CELEBRATION OF THE GOSPEL THAT THE PROCLAMATION AND DEMONSTRATION OF THE GOSPEL WILL INCREASE.

The Holy Spirit desires to again build habitations for God's presence to manifest on earth. Yes, we will proclaim the gospel. Yes, we will demonstrate the gospel. And how much more should we as His people celebrate what we have been given and received through perpetual thanksgiving and praise?

This is the emerging move of God coming to the earth. It will take place in homes, businesses, huts, coffee shops, and churches. It will not be bound by a style or a method, a personality or genre of music, but by hearts that have been transformed by the grace and work of Jesus. It is through the right response and celebration of the gospel that the proclamation and demonstration of the gospel will increase.

We have seen countless lives transformed in environments where the template of David's tabernacle is being established. When God is praised, He is enthroned. When He is enthroned, His government increases on earth. These environments of praise create atmospheres where the hardest of hearts will soften, the unbelieving are made believers, and the coldness of religion is burned away in the fire of His intimate nearness.

The regular celebration of the gospel will take time to develop. Under David's leadership, a culture of worship and praise was established. David's tabernacle was not built overnight. It took time and immense sacrifice to establish. It was not one day a week, but every day and all day. Likewise, I believe we must open the church up beyond our Sunday morning services to allow for continual expressions of thanksgiving and praise—an invitation to continually celebrate the good news of the gospel.

Chapter 7

JESUS' LEADERSHIP > MAN'S LEADERSHIP

Jesus' leadership is greater than man's leadership.

There is an obvious leadership crisis in our day. The earth is longing for and seeking a leader, or to say it another way, the world is looking for someone to follow. From politics, to faith, to social media, to celebrities, we are seeking someone to follow.

The options are numerous, and the opinions are varied. The loudest voice usually gets the most attention and, if you draw a line, you will draw a crowd. The idea is not to simply share ideas but to tyrannize all competing ideas and parties.

Today, there is no lack of ideas to rally around, but it is the people with opposing ideas to the majority that are considered a problem and are villainized. We demonize our enemies and fall into any given echo chamber readily available to catch and console our victim-prone attitudes. Unfortunately, the church at large has taken the bait and any clear voice, attempting to offer liberating truth and clarifying wisdom, gets muddied within the cultural noise of the moment.

We are not facing the same challenges we did even a decade ago. The cultural slide into darkness, confusion, and deception is here, staying, and only increasing. Deception is here—it is crouching at our door, desiring to devour us. And deception is the distinguishing mark of the last days—when a leaderless society becomes swept away by a demonic and antichrist agenda.

This impending and volatile climate presents a crucial opportunity for us as leaders. God is raising up a new kind of leader to face these unique opportunities, and I don't want to falter or waver. I don't want me or you to become weary. I don't want our love to grow lukewarm.

The Kingdom of heaven is an undefeated Kingdom, continually victorious. King Jesus is Lord of the past, this present moment, and His leadership will prevail for all eternity. It is the active leadership of Jesus that is the greatest need in our day. I say active leadership because it is the only helpful prescription for the sickness that plagues our culture. We need an active move of His leadership in our nations—in our social, economic, political, educational, and religious systems.

His active leadership is different from His leaders. Jesus has amazing leaders who are operating in their God-given gifts and callings today. Romans 12:8 lists leadership as a gift endowed by the Father to men and women of faith. This gift is focused on leading and influencing others. While I applaud the many who have focused on the development of healthy leaders, I believe this simply is not enough to get us to where Jesus wants to take us. Our leadership of other men and women will not change the course of culture and reconcile systems back to Him.

Jesus is not looking for gifted leaders. Jesus is looking for humble servants who are surrendered followers to His leadership. The leadership of Jesus is different from man's leadership. Anyone can read a book about influence, impact, and leading men, apply those principles, and effectively see results, but still not be following the ways of Jesus.

You can actually be leading for Jesus yet not following Him. The nuance is important for us to understand if we are going to get to where He is wanting to take us.

The following list of competing emphases is my best attempt to distinguish between following Jesus as a leader and simply leading as a leader. While, in most cases, the listed pursuits are important, my proposal is that we rightly prioritize each emphasis if we want to experience the active leadership of Jesus in our ministries.

> JESUS IS NOT LOOKING FOR GIFTED LEADERS. JESUS IS LOOKING FOR HUMBLE SERVANTS WHO ARE SURRENDERED FOLLOWERS TO HIS LEADERSHIP.

Again, this is not a right and wrong but a primary and secondary approach to establishing Jesus's leadership. The column below lists the focuses I have identified in following the leadership of Jesus; the other focuses are on the traditional methods of reaching men through proven leadership principles. I am arguing, however, that to move heaven to earth and impact culture, we must be followers of one Man first. Jesus said, "Follow me, and I will make you fishers of people" (Matt. 4:19).

Jesus' Leadership	Man's Leadership
Fear of the Lord	Fear of Man
Presence	People
First Love	Second Love

Praise and Worship	Preaching and Teaching
Presence	Presentation
Immeasurable	Measurable
Heaven	Earth
Intimacy	Influence
Following Jesus	Leading Men
One Thing	Many Things
Grow in Grace	Grow in Gifts

FEAR OF THE LORD > FEAR OF MAN

In this first section, both pursuits are not needed. The fear of God will actually set us free from the fear of man. First and foremost, we must return to the fear of the Lord. The fear of the Lord is the most needed dimension of the manifestation of the Spirit (see Isaiah 11). Jesus delighted in the fear of the Lord. This posture before God will establish us rightly to lead and love men.

For too long, we have loved God and feared men—it is from the overflow of our love of God that has driven us into a frenzy of serving and reaching people. To that end, we have subtly made the exchange from serving men to fearing them. In the name of reaching them, we have catered to relevance and influence for impact. Their opinions and approval have too often driven us as leaders. Mike Bickle, founder of the International House of Prayer, said, "The church has been intoxicated with the approval of man for the last 20 years."

We are easily swayed by the latest social dilemma, justice cause, and news cycle. We feel the demand to speak up and speak out—but we count the costs and often shrink if it is counter cultural. This will end when we grow in the fear of the Lord.

Today, God is removing the fear of and need of approval from others. While most of the items on the chart above are important and need to be applied to our ministries, the fear of man is something we have zero need for. Ever. And especially in the days ahead. The fear of God will lead us to a truth-centered and liberating love for others. We will love God and truth over the approval of people.

PRESENCE > PEOPLE

The fear of the Lord will reprioritize the presence of the Lord. We will not settle for anything less than the manifest presence of Jesus. This won't simply be because of our vision and our theology. This will become the greatest reality that the church is known for—God's undeniable, tangible manifestation of His presence and glory.

The current state of the church in the West has a misnomer that overshadows this subject. I have personally encountered a great misunderstanding among church leadership: that if we make room for the presence of God in our communities, it will compromise our ability to effectively reach people. This is simply not true.

A primary way this misunderstanding has impacted our churches today is in our perspective of the corporate worship time during services. If we sing too long, people will not engage. If people don't engage, they will leave our church. If they leave our church, we are doing something wrong. Therefore, it is advised that we must not have corporate worship for too long—a tested and proven theory by the "experts" that church leaders are advised to follow if they wish to effectively reach people.

I disagree.

The church I currently lead is fourteen years old. Since its conception, we have not had a worship time last fewer than fifty minutes. This is not a rule, but a value that Lorisa and I have carried, and our congregants have now adopted. From the onset of our community, we established that worship is for, all about, and unto God. Our time devoted to singing to and about Him is a means for us to engage the presence of Jesus, both individually and corporately.

The purpose of singing our praise songs is not about people. We do not worship so that "people will get something out of it." By its very definition, worship is not for us; worship is for the Lord. It is a ministry for Him, unto Him, and solely about Him. Worship has an object, and for lovers of Jesus, the object of our worship is Him.

Other leaders often ask me, "How do you guys worship every service for so long? How do people actually stay engaged?" I have answered this question in various ways over the years. Yet, my favorite answer to this question came from my friend Michael Koulianos. Michael and his wife Jessica are the founders and pastors of Jesus Image Church in Orlando, Florida. It is very similar in heart and mission to UPPERROOM.

Many people ask Michael the same question about the worship culture at Jesus Image Church. He told me, "There is something off in their question. When we sing, we are not singing to people. Their names are not in the songs. The songs are not for them, about them, or to them. We need a fresh understanding of corporate worship."

He is absolutely right. The unified songs we sing to the Lord are a corporate expression of our collective love to Him. They are for Him. And

I believe corporate worship that is focused on the Lord is a primary way to start our services—inviting Him to come as the guest of honor and everyone present focused on His presence among us.

In my experience, this reaches and touches people more than we realize. For too long we have built our churches upon the doctrine we tout or messages we preach. Our theological positions or our latest series have been the driving force for our church and community culture.

Our messages are for the people. But the worship preceding the message is to be for the Lord. Because of our people-driven focus, the ministry for the Lord has too often been relegated to twenty minutes, and oftentimes the words sung are more about us and our feelings than about Him, His worth, beauty, or power.

> ALL WE VALUE MUST SUBMIT TO THE CHIEF VALUE OF HIS PRESENCE.

I remember a dear friend asking me years ago why I constantly talked about the presence of God. It sounded ethereal and "New Agey" to them. But rather than me talking more about it, I simply asked this individual to join me at a weekly prayer set. About thirty minutes into the prayer set, with tears in his eyes, he said, "Thank you. I understand now what you are talking about—thank you." He was encountering God's presence firsthand.

We can have everything yet miss the main thing. All we value must submit to the chief value of His presence. The value for right theology, Scriptural teaching, evangelism, gifts of the Spirit, leadership practices, and excellent programs, must be unto the value for His presence.

The psalmist states, "a day in Your courts is better than a thousand elsewhere" (Ps. 84:10). I love this scripture. We have songs declaring this reality, yet sometimes I must really ponder what the psalmist is saying—is it true that one day in the courts of the Lord is better than 1000 days anywhere else? Do I believe and live with that perspective?

Let's examine this verse a little more intently. The court of the Lord is His dwelling place. Psalm 100 says we enter His gates (access) with thanksgiving, and His courts (past the gates) with praise. So, gates give us access to the courts. We know the court to be a legal term, and in this case, the court of God is where the throne of God dwells. God is a judge, reigning from His kingly throne in His court.

In both cases, the psalmist is speaking of the dwelling abode of God's throne. Better is one twenty-four-hour period in His presence than 1000 days elsewhere.

Now 1000 days is just shy of three years in time (2.74 years). So, the psalmist is saying I would rather spend twenty-four hours in Your presence than three years anywhere else.

I don't know about you, but I love traveling. I have been to some of the most beautiful places on earth. From Hawaii to the Great Barrier Reef, to the Rocky Mountains, to the Middle Eastern shores of Dubai, and the central coast of Italy. I have also had the chance to meet a lot of amazing people. I have been in the homes of former presidents and had dinner with some heroes in the faith that I never thought I would have the chance to meet. I have been to famous athletes' homes and even had dinner with one of my favorite A-list movie stars in Beverly Hills.

Yet, the reality is, that three years in any of these places or with any of these incredible people does not compare to one day in the presence of the Lord. This is what scripture teaches.

As the presence of Jesus becomes our supreme value, I believe people will be impacted in unprecedented ways. We must see this focus as a means to reaching people more effectively than a model message or prescribed formula for corporate worship music. When Jesus' leadership is welcome, and He has time and space to speak, move, act, heal, convict, and redeem, He meets every need in the room.

The manifest presence of the Holy Spirit will provoke repentance and an awareness of a need for salvation. Over the course of thirteen years at UPPERROOM, we have seen countless people respond to an altar call in the middle of worship. That's right. In the middle of our allotted time of fixing our eyes on Him, we can see ourselves rightly, and therefore approach Him rightly as the remedy for every need, in every life, at any time.

Jesus is much easier to talk about when He is actually present. This pursuit does not negate preaching, teaching, and fellowship; it only accentuates it.

FIRST LOVE > SECOND LOVE

Loving the Lord first will reprioritize the presence of the Lord.

Loving Jesus is more important than loving people according to Jesus (Matt. 22:37-38). When asked directly, He defined for us in priority the two greatest commandments. The first, foremost, and greatest commandment is to love God. The second commandment is to love people. This order is important to note and important to ponder. We addressed this topic thoroughly in the previous chapter, but let's look at how it specifically relates to leadership.

> HE MEETS
> EVERY NEED
> IN THE ROOM.

First, we must acknowledge there is a distinct difference between these two commandments. They are not the same. While they work in tandem, they need to stand alone in our hearts. The love of God and the love of others are two distinct activities.

LOVE HAS A PLAN

Loving Jesus as a primary objective for a corporate body will begin to look like something distinct for us and the communities we lead. When actively and regularly obeyed, this commandment will have an expression. Beyond a value and understanding, we must have a plan.

For example, I love my wife. She is supreme to any other relationship in my life outside of the Lord. She is my "first" love when compared to any other earthly relationships and priorities. She comes before anyone and anything else.

This reality must be expressed to her. I can write about my love for her and tell everyone I know how much I love her, yet that would not be me actually loving her. Loving her must look like something *to her.*

Lorisa is a quality time person. She needs me to be present, engaged, and intentional in expressing my love to her. We have an evening once a week that is devoted to our relationship. We eat dinner together, connect, and share intimate details about our lives. We are typically affectionate both verbally and physically on this specific night.

Yet, this priority of loving her more than others must be expressed to her personally. I can verbally tell her of my love and demonstrate to her how much I love her by doing things for her, but without expressing my love to her through quality time and intentionality every week, I would not be loving her the unique way she receives love. Date night is sacred at the Miller household. It is the time and place where I get to express my love in word, deed, and connection to her directly. This night is how I protect, express, and experience my "first love" devotion to her.

LOVING GOD FIRST IS A SAFEGUARD

Also, keeping these commandments in proper order will safeguard you as a leader. As leaders, we know all too well how easy it can be to slip into unhealthy patterns of people pleasing. At the least, we become exhausted; and at the worst, we become burnt-out and embittered.

When we attempt to meet all the needs of others around us, answering all the questions, always casting vision, saying yes to every meeting, and supporting every idea and initiative... any time we would spend in the secret place is now cluttered with endless belabored problem solving, sermon prep, or intercession for others. When people are touched and moved by our leadership, we are on cloud nine. If the response is lackluster, we are down in the dumps.

In this scenario, our identity (and attitude) rises and falls week to week at the whim of what others say and feel about us. We have lost the intimacy of communing one on one with the Father and letting Him establish and sustain our identity.

All the while, the Father invites us to sit at the feet of His Son—to become refreshed as we love Him, and not weary of doing good. He is waiting and wanting to prune everything that is draining us of the abundant life and fullness of joy we are promised in Him.

We can preach about how He is the source, the fountain of life, but we so easily lead others and our churches as if we are expected to be that fountain of life for everyone. We unknowingly step onto the platform, unintentionally becoming the "solution" that God's people look to, instead of enthroning and fixing our eyes on the One who promises to meet every need according to His glorious riches.

Regular realignment with the first and greatest commandment will breed healthy authority, longevity, and peace-filled, godly confidence as a leader. We do not lead for Him; we lead because we follow Him.

As pastors and church leaders, we must grapple with how this commandment is corporately obeyed and infiltrated through our communities. How do we practically love God together? We must seek revelation and get gripped by a conviction of loving God together in a corporate expression.

The first commandment must be more than a verse shared, exhortation, or sermon topic. It must "grow legs" and be practically walked out day in and day out in our communities. This activity cannot be assumed, it must be put into practice. As leaders, we must model this before others. Like Paul, can we say, "Be imitators of me, just as I also am of Christ" (1 Cor. 11:1)?

Loving God corporately looks like something very intentional and expressed in our services and prayer sets. Most commonly, we love Him through regularly giving thanks and praise, reading and praying scripture, through uniting in song, and taking communion together—corporately remembering His death and resurrection.

PRAISE AND WORSHIP > TEACHING AND PREACHING

In my experience, praise and worship reaches and touches people more than we realize. For too long we have built our churches upon the doctrine we tout or messages we preach. Our theological positions or our latest series have been the driving force for our church and community culture.

Our messages have been for the people. But the worship preceding the message is to be for the Lord. Because of our people-driven focus, the ministry for the presence of the Lord has been relegated to twenty minutes, and oftentimes the words sung are more about us and our feelings than it is about Him, His worth, beauty, or power.

Not everything in this chapter or listed on the chart is an either/or scenario. And especially for this specific topic, we must embrace the "both/and."

However, it is important we focus on the purpose of corporate worship. This question has formed the mission of our local community and church. We exist to minister to the Lord, morning, noon, and night. While we do this as individuals, we have also corporately decided to create a daily rhythm for ministry to the Lord. This is our "legs" for our first-love ministry.

We intentionally minister to the Lord with worship and prayer daily, from 6:00 – 8:00 a.m., 12:00 – 2:00 p.m., and 6:00 – 8:00 p.m. We have hundreds of volunteers gathering in a (mostly empty) room to minister to and love the Lord. This activity has established a culture where praise and worship have been at the center of all that we do.

In a weekend church service, this daily rhythm of our worship and praise culture "shows up." While we teach and preach for an hour during most weekend services, we know this is not the primary reason we gather. We gather as a church family first to love the Lord through giving Him our praise and worship.

Teaching then follows this activity of praise and worship. Biblical teaching is certainly vital to our young community, but it is not the centerpiece. It serves and aids that mission, but it is not the mission. Worship is for Jesus and the message is for His people. And we need both for our community to be healthy.

Heaven is marked by song, with music surrounding the throne. For the rest of time, we will praise and worship as an eternal occupation. When we do this together as a community here on earth and this side of heaven, the Spirit of God roots and establishes us in this eternal identity. From the baby in the womb, to the elderly, to the mentally disabled, all of creation exists to worship and give glory to God. We were created by Him, are sustained through Him, and our whole existence is unto Him. The activity of worship is necessary, principal, and foremost to any other thing we do.

This is the primary biblical prescription I see for loving God. While we can do it in other ways, the primary expression is song, sounds, and unified prayers. In collective worship, we behold the One we are enthroning in our praise. As we behold Him, we as a community, adore, love, worship, bow, and commune with Him.

A funny thing happened a few months into us releasing our worship moments online. As we were all in awe of how impactful these moments were to the body of Christ at-large, I was intrigued by how we titled our videos. It seemed that every video we posted had the word "spontaneous" in parentheses. I was confused by the description and especially that every song had the word "spontaneous" next to it. So, I asked my team the obvious question: "What is up with the word spontaneous on every video?"

They told me this is the genre of worship that our worship music fits into. People search for prophetic or "spontaneous" moments, and this helps the YouTube algorithm identify our content.

I responded, "Well, if it's spontaneous then why is the word on EVERY one of our videos? That doesn't seem very spontaneous!"

They laughed and I laughed, but my point was valid. My suggestion to our team was that we start a new genre of worship called "relational" worship. Instead of us "spontaneously" singing, people need to understand that what naturally bubbles up in song by one of our leaders—perhaps as a prayer, or chorus, or phrase—is a relational response to personally encountering the presence of the Lord.

The word spontaneous denotes something haphazard or occurring by chance, yet I don't think that is an accurate description of what actually happens during our times of worship. As a team, we have studied the leadership of Jesus for Jesus. We have learned, and are continuing to learn, how to respond to His entry. The songs, prayers, declarations, and "spontaneous" choruses are a heart response to His presence manifesting. They often lead to a corporate time of intercession or ministry to one another.

Worship is how we corporately and collectively love and respond to Him. As leaders, we must teach our worship teams, singers, and musicians the importance of welcoming and yielding to God's presence in the assembly of saints. When His presence comes, does He stay? When He stays, what does He want to do? And do we as leaders yield to His desires?

PRESENCE > PRESENTATION

David danced before the ark. The entry of the ark into Jerusalem was a day that was unlike any other in the history of Israel. Not only was the ark entering back into the capital of Israel, but a king was leading the procession for its entry.

Yet, this celebration was not appreciated by all. David's response to the ark provoked a response from his wife Michal. She confronts the king because she was confronted by the king's radical display. His dancing before God's ark was not appropriate by her measure. A royal member, much less her husband and Israel's king, should not have been so publicly undignified before the people. She felt reproach, embarrassment and offense at her husband.

In her reproach to him, we learn something about David. Michal was focused on the people's perspective of his leadership. *You undressed yourself of your royal robes in front of the maidservants and commoners.* Yet David was not dancing for the people. David was dancing before God. "It was before the Lord, who chose me above your father and above all his house, to appoint me ruler over the people of the Lord, over Israel; therefore, I will celebrate before the Lord. I will be more lightly esteemed than this and will be humble in my own eyes..." (2 Sam. 6:22-23).

This uncovering was before the eyes of God, not the eyes of people. His 'un-presentation' of himself as a king was because of the Lord's entry among the people. David was essentially saying, "I will become unpresentable in the presentation of God Himself." As their leader, David was modeling a right response to the presence of the Lord through his dancing and celebrating.

His lavish worship of the Lord also resulted in him lavishing, yet practically, blessing the people. David blessed all in the service that day by giving them goods–cakes, dates and raisins. He blessed them with provision in the procession of God's entry. This is typical of God's presence entering into a place and space–blessings abound.

In verse twenty, we read another interesting detail to David's celebratory worship and blessing. The king had just blessed the nation, and he entered his home to also bless his wife and household. I can only imagine that one way he was coming home to bless his home was to lay with his wife. I am reading into this a bit so forgive me, but one way for Michal to have received a blessing from David would be to bear his children. A child from David would ensure the legacy of both David and ultimately

Michal's family, which would have been Saul's lineage. Yet, because of her heart's posture of offense and reproach towards David's undignified response to God's entry, she judged him. She did not honor the leadership of her king and husband as he was 'humble in his own eyes' before the presence of the Lord.

The passage concludes that Michal was barren because of this incident. David coming home to bless his household resulted in a curse upon his wife. She postured herself in offense towards David and ultimately towards God. She missed the holiness and magnitude of the moment, that if appropriately received could have produced generational blessing.

> "I WILL BECOME UNPRESENTABLE IN THE PRESENTATION OF GOD HIMSELF."

My concern today is that we have taken a similar view towards God's presence. God's presentation of Himself oftentimes requires us to be unpresentable. The unveiling of God's presence in a corporate setting oftentimes disrupts and disturbs our preferences, plans and presentations.

One of the tensions I face in the current church leadership models is that we are way too pretty. The predictable, polished, structured presentations on Sundays will rightly be challenged if the manifest presence of God is to be central to the church. It is not that they are wrong, but that they are not enough and certainly not the point. His house is to be a dwelling place for His presence, and His presence is to be the focal point of His house.

David was dancing as a worshiper not as a king that day. David's kingship was humbly laid aside and submitted to the Kingship of God at that moment. God taking his rightful place in Jerusalem resulted in David leading the nation to rightly responding to God's leadership in the moment.

This was not about David presenting himself as king, but rather about God being presented as King of Israel, the King of kings. This resulted in David voluntarily laying his dignity before God. May leaders emerge today who will do the same.

IMMEASURABLE > MEASURABLE

It is natural and normal that people, and especially leaders, feel a sense of productivity and success when we see positive measurables. We love to measure how our efforts result in outcomes: chairs, budgets, clocks, services, attendance, views, clicks, memberships, salvations, offerings, volunteers, followers, etc. We like to weigh it, touch it, feel it, and know our metrics.

But the measuring stick is changing. God is ready to lead us into the immeasurable.

How challenging is it to measure the presence of God? In the early days of our community, God stripped me of the metrics. We had no media, no website, no podcast, no YouTube, and no data collection of attendance or giving. The one measurable we had was a few weekly prayer meetings. Even then, there was nothing to measure, because hardly anyone came.

We opened our doors every morning, noon, and night. For three years, the average attendance that came during the week was perhaps ten people. Most of the time, it was me and my spiritual momma, Jane, sitting in the corner, praying.

It was during this season that I began to measure success differently. The one growing question I had in my heart was this: Did God show up? When He came, did He stay? When He stayed, did I yield? This too was incredibly hard to measure. After all, how do you measure God showing up? This would be the great experiment that eventually became what the UPPERROOM is today.

Over time, the markings of His presence among us, and our response did become more recognizable and oftentimes tangible. Ironically, this often, if not always, negatively impacted the other metrics leaders typically like to employ to measure impact—like people leaving, not engaging, getting bored, and not understanding what was happening.

Eventually, I became okay with this. It took time (and the death of my traditional leadership desires to people-please), but I knew He was the goal and that He was teaching me about His leadership. Eventually, the measurables happened—yet in an immeasurable fashion. We got to experience His leadership.

> DID GOD SHOW UP? WHEN HE CAME, DID HE STAY? WHEN HE STAYED, DID I YIELD?

Let me give a real-life example. For about seven years, we had almost no media presence; just a landing page with our address, a map, and the hours for our prayer room and services. After seven years, at the Lord's very clear leading, we, with fear and trembling, began to share small moments of our culture on YouTube. I would describe these moments as God's manifest presence—moments our little community had been enjoying and stewarding for years but had intentionally never publicized.

When we first started to post on our YouTube channel, it seemed that overnight we had hundreds of thousands of followers. We had been on a journey of following Him together for years, and we went from spending hours in intentional hiddenness to sharing our culture of worship and ministry to the Lord with the online world.

That was in 2017, seven years after first starting morning, noon, and night prayer and worship sets. Since 2018, our church has had a few hundred people waiting up to two hours prior to any given weekend service outside in the unpredictable, and often sweltering, Texas weather. Every space we have found in Dallas, God has filled. Unfortunately, some people have even stopped attending because there simply is such limited parking and seating available. I am a father of four young kids, and it is understandable that families with small children would not wait in a line outside for two hours. I certainly wouldn't.

From monies raised, to media impact, to salvations and other valuable metrics, we have far exceeded anything we could have attempted to accomplish in our own wisdom or strength. This is solely the fruit of His leadership coming and His presence dwelling and remaining with us. May God help us to never get distracted by the measurables as the immeasurable One continues to make Himself known in our midst.

HEAVEN > EARTH

Heaven is much more relevant than we realize. Heaven is our home, and we are living for and unto heaven being established on earth. A renewed mind is a heaven-centered mind. As the Bible says, our identity and citizenship are heavenly. We are seated in Christ in heavenly places (Eph. 2:6).

When Jesus taught His disciples to pray, He taught them to say, "Your kingdom come, your will be done, on earth as it is in heaven" (Matt. 6:10). Our prayer, our worship, and our teaching must begin with heaven's realities. As leaders, we must position those we lead to see, think, and feel from heaven's perspective. If we begin from an earthly perspective, we will pray, worship, think, and feel from our own limited viewpoint, a carnal one. When we begin with heaven, we are positioned to operate from our proper vantage point as citizens of heaven.

The heavenly perspective will fuel missions on the earth. The book of Matthew tells us that before the return of Christ comes, the gospel of the Kingdom must be proclaimed to all nations. This understanding of the "last things" has led to an explosion of mission initiatives to reach every tribe, tongue, and nation.

> HEAVEN WON'T BE A PLACE IN THE AFTERLIFE, BUT A GROWING REALITY IN THIS LIFE.

As the return of Jesus draws closer, the church will refocus on heaven and the second coming of Jesus; it will be normative in the latter days. The Spirit and the bride will cry out for the return of Jesus. A holy ache of longing and desire for heaven will awaken in the souls of born-again believers. Heaven won't be a place in the afterlife, but a growing reality in this life.

INTIMACY > INFLUENCE

Intimacy with Jesus is much greater than influence with people.

As leaders, we must put influence in its proper place in our lives. Influence is a modern-day drug. The church, and especially we as leaders, have become intoxicated with being influential, relevant, popular, and liked. Now, more than ever, social media and smartphones have become bait for leaders to use the metrics of likes, clicks, and follows.

Influence in the Kingdom is not success. Kingdom influence is a fruit of intimacy. True spiritual fruit in the life of a believer is found in the secret place of intimacy we cultivate with the Lord. But spiritual influence is not equivalent to spiritual intimacy with Jesus. Just because someone is speaking for Jesus does not mean they are intimately following Jesus. Just because someone is leading for Jesus does not mean they are intimate with Him.

I have heard the Lord say to me, "Many are influential for me, yet not intimate with me." I shuddered in fear when I first heard Him whisper this in my spirit.

Jesus, even today, still lives and leads from a place of intimacy with His Father. He is not aware of the exact time of His second coming. The Father is the only one who knows (Matt. 24:36). So, Jesus, who is King, is still living dependent upon the Father's will. It is what He did while walking the earth, it is what He still does, and it is what we must do as well. We must be dependent upon the Lord in all that we do.

FOLLOWING JESUS > LEADING MEN

Not to belabor this point, but I must reiterate: Jesus is not a means to anything else. He is the goal. He is the point. Jesus is the destination.

Our leadership is the fruit of this reality. Jesus is not looking for you to do anything other than follow His leadership. He is looking first for followers. Disciples. Those who surrender and follow Him daily.

To grow in leadership is not the reason we follow Jesus, it will be the fruit of following His leadership. Anointing is great, but obedience is better. From the parable of the seeds, we see that only one in four soils produces lasting fruit. Even within that group, there were varying measures of fruit. Therefore, it can be argued that one out of four people will bear eternal fruit.

The same could be said of the 500-plus people who saw Jesus after His resurrection (1 Cor. 15:6). Can you imagine what it must have been like to have seen the resurrected Lord in person? The One who was publicly crucified and killed, alive and in front of you?

I am not sure what He told everyone that He saw, but I am assuming He reiterated to all that they must wait in Jerusalem for the Holy Spirit. It had to have been something He willingly shared over and over again.

Yet at Pentecost, when the Holy Spirit came, there were not 500 people in the original upper room. There were only 120. If you are good at math, and you divide 500 by 120, you get the one-quarter principle. Of the 500, only 24 percent of all who saw the resurrected Christ were waiting in the upper room.

"MANY ARE INFLUENTIAL FOR ME, YET NOT INTIMATE WITH ME."

I have pondered where the other 380 people were at Pentecost. Maybe they had previous commitments, slept in, were having breakfast...I don't know. Maybe some of them were out making disciples? Afterall, Jesus' departing words were, "Go into all the world and make disciples..." Could some have already moved into the place of active mission without Jesus sending the Spirit to source them?

Here's what I do know for certain: the church was birthed by the outpouring and leadership of the Holy Spirit. It was the power of the Spirit that led the disciples from the upper room to the southern temple steps, where 3,000 people were saved. Peter, who preached the first sermon after the outpouring of the Spirit, responded to the movement of the Spirit, and reached the nations. This was far beyond what they could have planned or strategized in the natural. The same is true for us—following

Him, and being filled and led by His Spirit, is preeminent to leading others to Him.

ONE THING > MANY THINGS

Pastoring is complex. I know the demands and pressures facing me, and any church leader, are daunting. Many eventually leave ministry due to these complexities. Culture is becoming ever more hostile to the gospel and truth, and therefore, hostile toward pastors who stand on and state the truth of the gospel. Instead of attempting to meet the ever-changing needs of today's culture, my suggestion is that church leaders simplify.

I believe simplicity is the key to longevity and, therefore, key to our efficacy as leaders. The simpler we get, the more effective we become. However, the word simple is not synonymous with the word "easy." Simplicity is actually very challenging to maintain. This is why I think we must get back to the one thing—the first and greatest commandment.

This was the secret to King David, Mary of Bethany, and the Apostle Paul. Each makes reference to the one thing desired, needed, and acquired: it is Jesus, and Jesus alone. On the surface, this seems like a no-brainer. "Come on Miller, of course it's all about Jesus. That's why we are doing what we do!" Yet is it the one thing you are known for? Is it what your friends or your church body would say about you?

Psalm 27 gives us valuable insight into what it means to pursue the one thing. David is facing every known problem a king could face—war, betrayal, sickness, fear, dread, and rejection from his family. In the middle of all of that, David cries out to God, and the request within his cry is fascinating to me. It would be a reasonable time to cry out, "Help!"

or, "God, send wisdom," or, "Rescue me!" But he doesn't ask for any of these things; he asks for one thing. "One thing I have asked from the Lord, that I shall seek: That I may dwell in the house of the Lord all the days of my life, to behold the beauty of the Lord and to meditate in His temple" (Ps. 27:4).

David knew then what I am calling you to remember now. The answer to every issue we possibly could face is discovered in the pursuit of this one thing: to behold Him, to minister to Him, to seek Him, to see Him rightly, and to worship Him. As leaders, we will do the body of Christ a disservice if we lay any lesser pursuit before those we lead. As leaders, we must first look to Him and lead others to do the same.

GRACE > GIFTS

This is a tricky one. As other values I have detailed in this chapter, it is not an either/or option. It is a both/and scenario. Yet, my proposal to us is that one must proceed the other for us to be most effective.

In ministry, whatever grows the church will sustain the church. While writing this book, I am concluding a four-month sabbatical. I have not been to a church service, staff meeting, or even checked my work email in sixteen weeks. It has been incredible (and extremely challenging).

Lorisa and I had our first re-entry call last week with our elders. The most common comment I hear from most people at the church, including the elders, is how much they miss us relationally. Yet, everyone has said that the church has not missed a beat since our departure.

"We miss you relationally, of course, but the church just seems to be thriving in your absence."

For some, comments like this would make them feel disrespected, not needed, or insecure. Not us. We are genuinely comforted—rejoicing and fully aware that this endeavor we call UPPERROOM has been, is, and forever will be God's doing. You see, we intentionally chose to not build upon a gift or personality, but only upon the grace God allotted to us. We fully believe God's grace, and the stewardship of it, has built our community.

While I use my gifts of preaching and leadership daily in our community, this has not been the focal point for our body. The foundation and focus have been the grace of God upon the mission and value we have of first hosting His presence and ministering to Him. The presence of Jesus is the reason our church has ever, and, I believe, will continue to experience growth.

While I actively work to develop and refine my preaching and leadership gifts, it is not the reason why our church has grown. Grace will use gifts, but it is not dependent upon them. While I, as a leader, grow and exhort those around me to also grow, we must first and foremost learn to grow in the grace of our callings.

The Bible says in Romans 11:29, "For the gifts and the calling of God are irrevocable." This means you can actually operate in your gifting and your calling void of connection to Him. He is so patient, kind and long-suffering. This verse speaks to the faithfulness of God and His abounding grace to those He has called (specifically Israel).

This is the point. If God has called you, He will fulfill that calling. We must trust and surrender to the grace of God to establish His house the way He designed. While I am the least gifted and anointed in many areas of ministry, I learned early on that gifting and anointing will only go so far. It is the grace of God that will take us, sustain us, and establish us far beyond our giftings and individual anointings.

Stewardship is crucial to understand, and it typically comes in the form of hardships, persecution, betrayals, setbacks, and shortcomings—and there we find grace, in the very midst of those trials. Trusting in that grace grows our authority to advance forward, through and beyond all the challenging and painful moments.

Grace is not just something we are saved by. It is the foundation of our faith and the source and sustenance of our calling. Any gift we have is from Him and serves the grace of our calling. Grace is the only thing that will forever sustain, grow, and establish us.

THE ACTIVE LEADERSHIP OF JESUS

I appreciate the wisdom and various focuses on leadership training that resources pastors and faith leaders today. However, principles and skills are simply not enough in the critical days that await us. We must elevate the active leadership of Jesus on the earth today.

The cultural challenges are not ceasing. The nations will rage against the leadership of Jesus and His people (see Psalm 2). The church will become more and more counter-cultural and persecution normalized. As leaders, we must prepare for that hour now.

In answering the disciples' question about the signs of His second coming, Jesus gave a sobering warning: "See to it that no one misleads you. For many will come in My name, saying 'I am the Christ,' and they will mislead many people" (Matt. 24:4-5). Again, He states, "Many false prophets will rise up and mislead many people" (Matt. 24:11).

It is amidst the issues of the last hours that people will be looking for a leader and be vulnerable to being misled. The cultural demands and pressures will create a leadership vacuum for the nations that the spirit of the Antichrist seeks to fill. We must have faith leaders who are first and foremost actively following and fortified in the leadership of Jesus.

The above priorities will help guide Christian leaders to yield to the active leadership of Jesus. The Holy Spirit will source us with strategies, initiatives, and wisdom in the last hours. But it is pressing that we discipline ourselves now in how to yield and be led by Him. The end times will be one of the darkest hours for people, yet one of the brightest hours for the church. His leadership will be crucial and His leaders that seek His active leadership will be equipped and ready.

Chapter 8

HOUSE OF PRAYER

By this point, I pray you have felt the invitation and conviction to review and align your leadership and calling with the priorities of God we see outlined throughout scripture. He is to be preeminent—not only in theory, but in practice. Now, it is time to address His temple-city, His house, His church, His place of worship. It is time to take an honest look at what He definitively says about His church and humbly ask His Spirit to help us to obey His word. Foundation repair may be needed. It is costly, but the alternative will be even more costly.

Before we continue, take a moment to ask Him to give you eyes to see, a humble spirit, and the courage to say "yes" to any way He may lead. May we be those who tremble at His word (Isa. 66:2), not out of fear, but out of reverent obedience that He, and His word, are the only way, truth, and life for us.

It may take some rewiring for us to learn about the house of God, according to God. Jesus was passionate, clear, and unequivocal when He described His house. He did not mince words. With great zeal, he quoted the prophet Isaiah, "My house shall be called a house of prayer" (Matt. 21:13).

He said that His home will be a home marked by one activity: prayer. If you come into a place where people are praying, you know that my house has been established. Where prayer happens, I will live and dwell.

Now, if you're like me, you probably have a preconceived notion of a "house of prayer." In fact, in our modern Western evangelical lens, there is a generally accepted construct for a house of prayer that we perceive to be very different from how we understand church today.

At UPPERROOM, we often are asked, "Is UPPERROOM a church or a house of prayer?" This well-meaning question is quite revealing of our misunderstanding of what Jesus said about His house. According to Him, His church is a house of prayer. A house of prayer is not for a radical few. It is not solely for missionaries, intercessors, the retired elderly with time on their hands, or unemployed young people. It is for all His body, all His church, in all places, and at all times.

Now, let me ask you, if you survey the activities happening today in "His house," where would prayer rank? While I think most churches and ministry leaders have a value for prayer, is it the defining activity for His house? Reflect upon the last time you gathered with Jesus followers in one location—was prayer the primary and defining activity?

This description of His house is the greatest invitation for us as His people to explore if we are willing to be malleable in the journey and yielded in the discovery. What was in His heart when He said that this one activity—prayer—will mark the people who dwell in His house?

PRAYER IS RELATIONSHIP

Definitions are important. When I say the word prayer, it could be defined in a number of ways. If I ask you and two other people, "How do

you define prayer?" there is a good chance all three would give different definitions attempting to describe the same word. Prayer is talking
to God. Prayer is intercession. Prayer is requesting something from God.
Prayer is _____ (fill in the blank).

How would you define prayer? It is an elastic word; it can be stretched
to mean a number of things to a number of people. For our understanding of the word, I want to bring a clear and concise definition to prayer.
For our community, it has been imperative for us to hear and agree on the
same thing when we use this word.

At UPPERROOM, prayer is defined as relationship. When I read
the word prayer, I read the word relationship. Relationship is a two-way
exchange between people talking, listening, engaging, connecting, and
responding to one another through dialogue.

A house of prayer is a house in active, ongoing, communicative relationship with God. Therefore, a group of people in relationship with
Jesus is His desire and the mark of His house. And a house of prayer
(church) is a group of people that have learned to commune with, hear
from, speak to, and respond to Jesus.

This exchange is a learned one that takes time, energy, and much discipline. This definition of prayer as relationship has come over time to
me, our leadership, and now our entire church body as we have explored
why Jesus described His house in this way.

A HOUSE THAT PRAYS

What did He mean when He said, "My house will be a house of prayer"?
Think of it as a glorious red carpet for His people to take His description
of His house quite literally. His house will be marked by people engaging

Him in prayer. In this invitation, Jesus requires humility to discover what He desires when He describes His house as a place of prayer.

Prior to my personal experience at UPPERROOM, I had no desire to know or understand what this meant—even as a faithful believer on staff at a church. Literally, I thought Jesus' description was intended for individuals and a directive that we should regularly be talking to Him. I personally prayed; taught people to pray; and prayed with others before, in between, or after organized meetings, activities, and meals. Yet, the purpose of the gatherings I attended was not to pray. It was to meet, eat, or do something. The intention to gather was never for the sole purpose of prayer.

> AT UPPERROOM, PRAYER IS DEFINED AS RELATIONSHIP.

I cannot think of a regular time when I, along with any other seminary colleagues or church leaders, talked through what it meant to define our churches or structure our gatherings with prayer as a priority. But Jesus said it, and not subtly. Although it was never a topic of discussion in any class or church, I was part of, I am convinced the global bride is long overdue to begin exploring what it means for our churches to be houses of prayer.

Of course, prayer is an activity that we all believe in. It would be hard to find anyone, believers and nonbelievers alike, that don't have some value for prayer or divine communion. In the church, prayer is an essential discipline and activity that everyone universally agrees we should be doing. And although we believe in the power and purpose of prayer today, why is it that so few communities target this sole activity as the ultimate purpose for gathering?

WORSHIP IS CENTRAL

I was with a group of pastors recently whom I love and respect. They were discussing a recent study put out by a leading church planting network that is advising pastors to not worship more than twenty-one minutes in a Sunday service gathering. According to the research they collected, they presented data that nonbelievers disengage after that allotted time. And if they disengage prior to the sermon, then they will not hear the gospel message. If they do not hear the gospel message, then we are not fulfilling the Great Commission. We have a responsibility to win the lost, and therefore, they are convinced the activity of worship for longer than twenty-one minutes hinders the Great Commission mandate.

These pastors, along with countless others, have made adjustments to their services, trimming down worship so the sermon can be the focal point of their church gathering.

My heart was so grieved as these pastors shared this with me, I actually began to weep at our lunch. I was not crying for them and their communities, I was weeping because of what it reveals about us and our priorities. Over time, we, as leaders of His house, have tragically exchanged His desire, definition, and strategy for His house with our own strategies for His house.

I understand the data and I believe the data is logical, as the church exists today. The data is not wrong, but our response to the data is wrong. Again, if Jesus said His house will be defined by this activity—was He not aware that people who did not know Him would be in His house? I am certain He did know that. And knowing nonbelievers would come to His house, He still did not compromise His description of His house as one of prayer. So, the question at hand is how do churches reach the unbelieving by prioritizing an activity that they don't understand or believe in—prayer?

In the last fourteen years of leading the UPPERROOM, we have committed to the house of God being defined by the activity of prayer. The daily participation in this activity has created a culture that has established our house and is now normal—daily prayer and worship is occurring.

Every church community has some measure of prayer and worship activities already happening. Yet, are they the defining activities of their church culture? I believe this is what Jesus is addressing. The culture of heaven is one of worship and prayer. Therefore, the culture of the church should be the same. "My house will be called a house of prayer" (Matt. 21:13).

Establishing this culture has been the most challenging, gut-wrenching, and glorious endeavor I have ever done. Honestly, there have been times I wish Jesus would have said His house was defined by another activity. I could pull off creating a house of preaching, a house of evangelizing, a house of discipleship, a house of fellowship, or other employed strategies for His people gathering in His house. Yet, Jesus said His house will be a house of prayer. As I said in chapter one, this endeavor was a personal graveyard, the utter death of myself.

HOLY WEEK

It is helpful to carefully examine the context and narrative surrounding the Lord's description of His house in Matthew 21. It begins with the triumphal entry on Palm Sunday and continues with Jesus cleansing the temple. The triumphal entry gives us insight into the mindset of the people welcoming Him and what Jesus was communicating as He entered the temple that Holy week.

He entered on a donkey. He was the coming King that the people (and history) had awaited, for centuries. He was fulfilling prophecy as He rode into the religious epicenter of Jerusalem. He came with a king's welcome as the people shouted "Hosanna to the Son of David; Blessed is He who comes in the name of the Lord; Hosanna in the highest!" (Matt. 21:9).

This procession caused quite an uproar in the city. Everyone was aware that Jesus had entered the city because the occasion stirred a buzz of energy and conversation throughout the city. In verse 10, it states that the entire city was asking one question, "Who is this man?" From the coffee shops to the marketplace, to the neighborhoods to the courthouse, the entire city was moved by Jesus—yet unsure of who He truly was.

Is He a prophet? Messiah? Rabbi? A heretic? Who is this person causing such a stir? The stories and testimonies had circulated. He heals the sick. He raises the dead. He multiplied food and turned water into wine. He says He is God. He is a lunatic. He is leading a cult. He is going to overthrow Caesar and the Roman reign. He was the talk of the town, and, at that moment, the Bible says that the ENTIRE city asked the most central question one can ask— "Who is this?"

What does Jesus do? Jesus turns to His house, the temple. He enters His home that the patriarchs of old had built—a place where His Father, and therefore Himself as the Son, would be known, understood, honored, and celebrated. He has an expectation of that house, and what He finds is clearly not consistent with His expectation. He came looking for those positioned and eagerly ready to receive Him—those who could answer, "Who is this?" But this is not what He finds in His house.

Instead, He finds men and women busy being productive. Jesus comes into His house and finds His people busy with the production and consumerism of buying and selling. He is grieved and enraged at what He finds. On a separate occasion (John 2), we know that He strategically planned the cleansing of His temple as He made a whip intentionally to drive out those in charge of His house. In this account, He targets the tables where trade is being made and He turns them over.

It is in this context that Jesus makes His emphatic statement, quoting the prophets Isaiah and Jeremiah, "It is written, 'MY HOUSE SHALL BE CALLED A HOUSE OF PRAYER'; but you are making it a robbers' den" (Matt. 21:13).

What was His expectation? What was His desire for His house upon entering it? He explicitly says that the mark of His house will be prayer. It goes without saying, then, that His house would be marked by people in relationship with Him—talking to and receiving from Him, and offering sacrifices of thanksgiving, praise, and worship. The mark of His house will be people who are in right relationship with Him, ready and waiting for Him when He comes.

I hope if you were to enter my house you would learn a lot about me. By just being inside my house, you would be able to learn about me and the things I care about. You would see my love for my children through the photos of them, their art displayed, their toys and games. You would see my value for good coffee and food. You would be able to tell I like golf by my clubs, my hats, and looking in my closet. Without me being present, if you were to enter my house, you would be able to surmise a good deal about me.

Likewise, Jesus was entering His house expecting that what was within would point to WHO He is—and answer the very question the people were asking outside the temple. The entire city was stirred, asking a question, and Jesus looked to His house to answer. I believe a community that has become His house is rightly establishing His heart and character for the world to see and know who our God is. The purpose of His House is to reveal the One who dwells there. When people enter our churches, have we made it obvious who Jesus is?

REMOVING THE LEAVEN

Recently I had the opportunity to go to Jerusalem with a dear friend of mine, Rabbi Jason Sobel. When visiting the Temple Mount, we were leaving the Southern Steps and heading to the Western Wall. At the southwest corner of the Temple Mount, they were excavating the area right outside the place where the temple was during Jesus' time. Recent discoveries have found an ancient marketplace, with evidence of trading tables, shekels, and products like pottery, dishware, and other historical relics.

THE MARK OF HIS HOUSE WILL BE PEOPLE WHO ARE IN RIGHT RELATIONSHIP WITH HIM, READY AND WAITING FOR HIM WHEN HE COMES.

As Rabbi Jason pointed this out, I was reminded of Jesus' declaration inside the temple where He defined His house as a house of prayer. He made this declaration right after He turned the tables upside down and drove the money changers and vendors out of the temple. I asked Rabbi Jason about the narrative in Matthew 21; he had the most profound understanding, which adds great insight to this discussion.

Jesus made His declaration during the week leading up to Passover.

This would have been the busiest time of year in and around the temple in Jerusalem. Thousands of Jews would voyage to the temple to bring offerings, alms, and sacrifices to the temple for Passover. The tables within the house would have provided the means for these sacrifices to be obtained, since most people purchased these goods upon arrival into Jerusalem rather than traveling long distances with them.

We know those responsible for the temple had allowed it to be turned into a marketplace. At a surface level, it seems easy to understand why Jesus cleared the temple. Yet, there was something else happening during this time. During the Holy Week of Passover, there was a Jewish custom called Bedikat Chametz. This custom was to fulfill the command in the law from Exodus 12:15.

THE PURPOSE OF HIS HOUSE IS TO REVEAL THE ONE WHO DWELLS THERE.

Every year at Passover, children were commissioned by their parents to cleanse the home of all leaven. Many times, they would make it into a game where kids would be rewarded for finding any leaven within the home. As you know, leaven is the agent that influences bread to rise. It was a spiritual parallel for cleansing homes of any outside influences that had permeated the house.

When Jesus entered the temple, He was literally entering His Father's house. As kids across Jerusalem were cleaning out the physical leaven in their homes in preparation for the Passover, Jesus was cleaning out the spiritual leaven in His dad's house. He was removing the lesser influences that had begun to overshadow the most important influence (i.e., prayer, relationship). The production of the house to fulfill the duties of the house had eclipsed the very purpose of the house.

The purpose of the house was communion and right relationship with the Father. The production of doing things for God had overshadowed the purpose of the house—being in relationship with God. From Genesis onward, we know He desired a dwelling place on earth to be with His people. This is why Jesus said His house would be a house of prayer (relationship). The temple was a place to meet with, commune with, and be in right relationship with His people.

Jesus was, in essence, stating emphatically that His Father's house is to be a house where people are in relationship with His Father. No other activity is to overshadow, disrupt, or hinder people from communing with God. The purpose of the house is His Father resting in, abiding upon, and dwelling with His people. All activities should serve this end.

Is this true today? Do our churches place too much emphasis on production and duties rather than the simplicity of gathering for the sole intent of relationship with the Father?

Let me say it bluntly: all activities must serve this end. It is not that other activities are wrong, but they must be secondary to this primary activity of prayer that cultivates a relationship with the Father. In fact, I believe many activities will no longer be necessary when the simplicity of the primary activity is consistent in practice and established in the hearts and minds of His people.

As a pastor of His people, my goal is to create environments where people will learn how to individually and corporately be in relationship with the Lord. We learn to hear from Him, and we learn to speak to Him. The proclamation of the gospel, discipleship, community, and the likes must all serve this end. We rightly serve His house by teaching people to pray, and therefore be in relationship, with the living God.

GOD'S LIVING ROOM

As a young leader, the Lord began to provoke me with this idea of how He defined His house. I was a young adult pastor in Dallas, Texas. We were hosting a forty-eight-hour non-stop prayer meeting with musicians, worship, and prayer leaders leading two hour sets throughout the weekend. We had never done one of these before and really had no idea if it would "work"—whatever "work" meant.

I was leading a group of a few hundred young adults at a fairly progressive Church of Christ. The leadership had agreed to open our family life center (the church gym) for this weekend of prayer. We were about twelve hours into the event when I had the following conversation with a core team leader in our ministry—she was bringing her unbelieving cousin who had not darkened the doors of a church in over a decade.

"My cousin Steven has agreed to come. He has not been to church in over a decade. He is open to it because it's a prayer meeting and not preaching. He is a self-described agnostic, homosexual, who is visiting me from California. Could you meet us outside the church and help explain what we are doing to him before we come into the building?"

I agreed to meet them outside, not really knowing how to help Steven engage in a multi-hour prayer meeting. I appreciated my leader's faith in bringing him but was a bit skeptical about how her cousin would do in a prayer meeting—much less a prayer meeting that would last for another thirty-six hours.

You could immediately tell by the tank top, cutoff jeans, flip flops, and rainbow tattoo on his arm that Steven was not from North Dallas. He seemed to pride himself on his lifestyle and beliefs, and he also really loved his cousin. This was the reason he had agreed to come to her church.

After some small talk, I asked Steven if he wanted to come inside. He was apprehensive due to previous rejection and hurt from pastors at previous churches. He was open to the idea of coming to this church because his cousin assured him no one would be "preaching at him."

I assured him there would be no preaching, but I did say there would be singing and praying. I asked him to imagine God had invited Him into His home. God's expectations of Him were to make himself at home. Sit back, listen, observe, and let God host you in His home. "Imagine you are walking into God's living room for the next hour or so—just let Him be Him and you be you. Let's see what happens."

To be honest, as the leader of this event, I was a bit overwhelmed. This was a big weekend, trying something so new, and I was surprised by how many people turned out throughout the event. I had some housekeeping duties to tend to and honestly did not think much about Steven after our introduction. But Jesus was eagerly anticipating Steven's entry.

It was several hours later when my young adult leader came to find me in the prayer room. She told me that Steven wanted to speak to me again. So, I made my way over to the couch that he had been sitting on for a few hours. To my surprise, Steven was teary-eyed and noticeably moved by what he was experiencing. As I sat down, he kept saying "I don't know what has been happening. I don't know what is happening. Ever since I sat down and imagined God hosting me in His living room...I have felt an overwhelming sense of peace. I am overwhelmed by peace."

What I did not know about Steven was that he had a long-term bout with depression and anxiety. I told Steven that one of Jesus' names was Prince of Peace. "It is not surprising that you would experience peace when He is present." Steven started crying, and over the course of an hour, I shared the gospel with him. He gave His life to Jesus, and at the start of our evening weekend service later that day, Steven was water baptized. He sat through the entire service (including the preaching) and left the church that night a new person.

All of this happened because Steven attended a prayer meeting.

This was just one of a handful of testimonies that happened that weekend, and forever changed the trajectory of my leadership as a pastor. My initial curiosity had become a conviction. I now believe anything can happen when the manifest presence of God is His people's pursuit and priority.

Similar to us needing to define prayer as relationship, we as a community also needed to define "worship." We believe that worship is agreeing with who God says He is. When we worship (i.e., sing or pray truths about the character of God), people who are confused and questioning what God is like are hearing and being taught the nature of God. Corporate worship is the experience of a gathering of people confidently assured and proclaiming who God, the Father, Son, and Holy Spirit is—first to Him, but also to our spirits and minds. When we are communing with God, telling Him (and ourselves) who He is, we are declaring on earth what all of heaven already sees and knows. This is bringing the realities of heaven to earth. In worship that agrees with who God is and what He does, we are fulfilling the Lord's instruction in how to pray: "Your kingdom come. Your will be done, on earth as it is in heaven" (Matt. 6:10).

> WE BELIEVE THAT WORSHIP IS AGREEING WITH WHO GOD SAYS HE IS.

A HOUSE FOR HIS NAME

As I have described, the house of God is a place marked by His identity. In the Old Testament, we see how God commissioned Solomon to build Him a house—and we can find insight into God's desire and purpose in what He communicated to Solomon about His house. God specifically made it a point that Solomon was to build a house for His name.

At the dedication ceremony Solomon announces:

> Blessed be the Lord, the God of Israel who spoke with His mouth to my father David, and fulfilled it with His hands, saying, "Since the day that I brought my people from the land of Egypt, I did not choose a city out of all the tribes of Israel in which to build a house, so that My name might be there, nor did I choose any man to be the leader over my people Israel; but I have chosen Jerusalem so that My name might be there, and I have chosen David to be over My people Israel." Now it was in the heart of my father David to build a house for the name of the Lord, the God of Israel. But the Lord said to my father David, "Because it was in your heart to build a house for My name, you did well that it was in your heart. Nevertheless you shall not build the house, but your son who will be born to you, he shall build the house for My name." Now the Lord has fulfilled His word which He spoke; for I have risen in place of my father David and sit on the throne of Israel, as the Lord promised, and have built the house for the name of the Lord, the God of Israel.
>
> —2 Chron. 6:4-10

What is the significance of building a home for God's name? This detail is incredible from both Solomon's perspective and the Lord's. God was looking for a place where His name could be housed. What does that even mean? Why would God desire a habitation for His name? This gives incredible insight into the desire of God for His house. He desires to dwell in homes that rightly honor and know His name.

Well, what's in a name?

The name of a person or a thing is fundamental. Everyone and everything on earth is given a name. When one is born in any country, at any time, a name is designated for that individual. A name marks the person for the remainder of their days. None of us chose the name we were given. If you wanted to change your name, you would have to legally take measures to do so.

One cannot go by one name today and another tomorrow. It would make no sense and be extremely confusing for anyone who had a relationship with you. Can you imagine if your name was constantly changing? Yesterday you were Tom and tomorrow you will be James. Today I am Michael Miller and tomorrow I am Tiger Woods. People would think you were crazy and probably distance themselves from you. People would not know who you are or what they should call you. "He was Tom yesterday but today He is going by James." NO. It's silly right? And this example is incredibly silly.

Yet this is what a lot of people do with the Lord. Because they do not know, or have not honored His name, they are not confident in who He is. There is a lack of revelation today around the knowledge of God. We have passively accepted that He is one thing to one person and another thing to another person. People are attempting to redefine Him based upon their personal experiences, feelings, or emerging beliefs, and not on His Word, which already accurately defines who He is.

Our belief about who God is lacks conviction and confidence because we have not built homes for His name.

God has clearly defined Himself in scripture. If we want to grow in the knowledge of who God is, we must have a revelation of the Name of the Lord. The church, or house of prayer (remember, they should be one in the same), is vital in establishing this reality on earth today. The church is to be for His name—the true and accurate experience and knowledge of who God is.

WORSHIP

A primary way we establish the name of the Lord is through worship. I told you that at UPPERROOM we define worship as agreeing with who God is. We have defined it in this way because that agreement in our hearts positions us to know Him rightly. Who we define God to be is the most crucial and formative revelation we will ever have. If you have a right understanding and knowledge of God, your life will line up with His will and His plans for your life.

> OUR BELIEF ABOUT WHO GOD IS LACKS CONVICTION AND CONFIDENCE BECAUSE WE HAVE NOT BUILT HOMES FOR HIS NAME.

The most important question we can answer is "Who do you say Jesus is?" This question is not a simple, onetime answer at an altar call; it is a lifelong and eternal discovery of His nature and character. Knowing Jesus intimately is the goal of the Christian life. This has to be at the center of all that we do and all that we seek—personally and corporately. He is the goal.

Growing up in the church, I did not have a clear understanding of who God defined Himself to be. Despite attending church multiple times every week, I was confused about God's nature and His character. My understanding of God from an early age was mixed between the Old Testament and the New. For the most part, my view of God was based on performance and behavior. If I did good, He was happy. If I was bad, He was forgiving but disappointed. My relationship with Him was based upon my response to Him. He changed as I changed. If I measured up to the perceived expectations I thought He had of me, then I was in His good graces. If I did not, then I would somehow have to earn my way back into right standing with Him. I had little understanding of His loving and gracious nature.

Our faith, and therefore our entire Christian journey in the Lord, must be rooted and grounded in a right understanding of His nature and character. We must be rooted in the truth of who God has revealed Himself to be in scripture. By the power of the Holy Spirit, when a group of people establish the reality of His name through worship, people will be transformed. This is not the sole purpose of His house, but it is foundational for its establishment to be for His name.

In Matthew 16, Jesus has an incredible conversation with His disciples. At this point in His ministry, He was attracting quite the following. He was the hot topic of conversation in and around Israel. The pressing question everyone was asking was, "Who is Jesus?" Jesus knew that even His disciples were entertaining the question among themselves.

He first asks them, "Who do the people say that I am?" Their answers varied, "Some say that you are Elijah, some Jeremiah, some compare you to the other prophets." This was the highest revelation that the people had of God. Yet, Jesus was setting up His disciples to see Him with fresh eyes. The disciples had left everything. They were "pot committed" to following the Lord, yet He knew they still had a limited revelation of who He actually was.

Jesus then asks His disciples the same question. It is one thing for other people to reveal God. It is another entirely for God to reveal God to you. This moment is so precious and significant for the disciples, and especially Peter. When Jesus asks this question, Peter, prompted by the Holy Spirit, says "You are the Christ, the Son of the living God."

Peter, for the first time, understands who Jesus is. He would not be limited to others' understanding or experience of God. Peter would have a firsthand encounter with the Holy Spirit's power to see and know the Lord rightly. The Father, by the power of the Holy Spirit, unveiled the true identity and nature of Himself in Jesus.

THE HOLY SPIRIT REVEALS JESUS

The Holy Spirit's favorite subject is Jesus. The Holy Spirit's role on the earth is to first and foremost reveal to humankind the knowledge of Jesus. This knowledge is inspired by God into the hearts of His people.

We must understand that we are dependent upon God to know God. This question "who do you say I am?" is being asked in this hour to the church—even to those who have known Him and walked with Him for a long time. He is inviting us through this question into a fresh revelation and understanding of Himself. The church (house of prayer) is the context where this question is repeatedly answered by His people as they establish a house for His name.

When the Holy Spirit reveals Jesus to us, it is as if we are learning what we have already learned for the first time. Over and over, we allow the Holy Spirit to lead us into the revelation of Jesus: His love, His faithfulness, His holiness, His kindness, His goodness, His power, His nearness, His joy, His peace, and on and on. The Christian life is unto this one end: the knowledge of God through the person of Jesus. As we behold Jesus, by the Spirit of wisdom and revelation, we are established in faith in the nature and power of our Lord.

JESUS IS INTRODUCING HIMSELF

Presence-led prayer will usher in the greatest worship movement, revealing who Jesus truly is to a dying and questioning world.

A few years ago, I was informed that a Muslim was going to attend the UPPERROOM. He had a business associate that was a member of the UPPERROOM, and he wanted to find a wife in America. This young man was from a prominent family in the Middle East. He was getting his MBA from a local university and was very interested in American girls. So, my friend brought him to the UPPERROOM. We have a young community, and he thought it would be a great way to get him around young Jesus-loving people.

> WE MUST UNDERSTAND THAT WE ARE DEPENDENT UPON GOD TO KNOW GOD.

His first visit was during our Sunday morning service. He was a bit overwhelmed the whole time, never having been to a Christian church. He was not engaged during worship and seemed to check out during the message. He did like the girls that he saw and was interested in how he could get back to the UPPERROOM to meet them personally. So, my friend told him about our prayer sets. We currently host prayer sets multiple times a day. The amazing thing about prayer is this man actually already prayed five times a day because of his faith in Allah. So, he thought, instead of going to the mosque, he would go to the UPPERROOM for prayer.

On this specific day, I was attending the prayer set when I saw this gentleman enter the prayer room. There were probably only ten to fifteen people there while a team of six volunteers led us in worship and prayer. The young man entered the room and sat on the very front row. He looked around for a bit and then closed his eyes and began to pray. Now, I don't know who he was praying to or what he was praying about, but about that time, a dear friend of mine who was leading the prayer set came off the stage and sat next to him.

She asked him if she could pray for him, and he said yes. I am not certain what she prayed but I do remember his response to the prayer. After a few minutes of her praying, I watched him take off his sports coat. Then he began unbuttoning his shirt and fanning his face due to "extreme heat all over his body" (as he would later describe).

My friend prayed, "You don't know Jesus, but today He is introducing Himself to you." At this point, the man fell on his knees and gave His life to the Lord. He described the experience, saying he had questions in his heart about who Jesus was, and in that moment, He knew Jesus was Lord and Savior.

That conversion happened in a prayer meeting. Someone questioning Jesus came into a room where His name was being honored and worshiped. From that environment came forth a revelation that would forever change his life. He was born again as a believer in Jesus through an environment of prayer and worship. Proverbs says, "The Name of the Lord is a strong tower; the righteous runs into it and is safe" (Prov. 18:10).

This is a primary way we establish God's house for His name today. Whether that be in our homes, our business, and especially our communities of faith, we need to establish the Lord's name as the only one that can save, the strong tower, the safety and powerful name that it is. We need to establish cultures of worship where we are rightly agreeing with who God is and what God is like. True worship accomplishes this. True worship rightly proclaims His nature and His character for others to encounter His nature and character.

QUALITY OVER QUANTITY

I have witnessed how the prayer movement can focus on the quantity of prayer occurring. The 24/7 model, which I applaud, is one way to rebuild the tabernacle. However, leaders have become paralyzed due to a tendency to overemphasize the quantity of time; instead, we need to focus on the quality.

Personally, I was extremely intimidated by the 24/7 house of prayer model. It seemed easy to fall in the trap of measuring success by the clock and how many hours of prayer a community was participating in. If you are not familiar with this model, then ignore this. But if you are, I implore you to please not get bogged down with how often you are praying. The number of hours or quantity of sets is not the goal. Jesus is our goal. Rightly hosting Jesus is our aim.

When I let go of the pressure to host nonstop prayer and worship, I was able to actually move toward hosting a few prayer and worship sets, beyond our weekly service, where we were pursuing the presence of God and worshiping consistently. It was sacrificial, but very doable. And as we grew faithful with a few sets, God's grace established our prayer and worship culture. Over time, the sets multiplied.

I cannot tell you how many hours, sets, or people are leading today across the various UPPERROOM churches. But I do know that because we started small, being faithful with a few quality sets, our people have a value for expecting the presence of God to come every time. We are corporately growing in how to respond to the leadership of His presence when He comes. Healthy prayer sets will

JESUS IS OUR GOAL. RIGHTLY HOSTING JESUS IS OUR AIM.

reproduce more healthy prayer sets. Healthy things multiply. Our quantity of sets has only been the byproduct of starting small and faithfully stewarding a few sets. As a leader, start small with a few like-minded and like-hearted others who desire to minister to the Lord.

MORNING, NOON, AND NIGHT

Our prayer rhythm at UPPERROOM comes from Psalm 55:17. I had read David's morning, noon, and night petition, and thought to myself, "that is a doable target for us as a church." Let's attempt to fill a room three times a day with thanksgiving, praise, and worship.

The most underused facilities in cities today are church buildings. We gather once a week in a building that typically sits empty the other six days a week. In addition to the resource of space, a house of prayer also provides a great opportunity to empower all hearts and gifts in your community. Not everyone is called to lead corporate worship on a stage in front of hundreds of people. Yet there are dozens, if not hundreds, of people in our communities that are called to minister to Him in a smaller context. Musicians, singers, poets, painters, and dancers are willing and called to serve Him in this manner. Do we have a conviction and vision to empower them?

Churches typically have space for a small handful of singers and musicians at a weekend service. But the Lord has gifted and anointed so many more to minister to Him in music and song. There is a disproportionate underutilization of these gifts and callings throughout the body of Christ, and a house of prayer creates an avenue for these gifts to be activated unto the Lord. The house of prayer that Jesus calls His church is a great invitation for us as His people to explore. We get to discover together what this mandate looks like in our day.

> PEOPLE REGULARLY BEING IN PROXIMITY TO THE PRESENCE OF THE LORD WILL TRANSFORM COMMUNITIES.

Howard Shultz, the founder of Starbucks, identified a niche for our cities and suburbs. In times past, homes were built with massive front porches. It was called the "third place" for life and community. Their place of business and homes were the first two. As we grew more industrialized and domesticated, we lost touch with our neighbors. Shultz desired to create an atmosphere where people would regularly gather with others around coffee in their neighborhoods. Starbucks coffee shops are our modern-day living rooms where life happens. He revolutionized communities by creating a comfortable "third place" for community to happen.

The house of prayer model could be another, even more powerful, "third place" for people to gather—one centered around the presence of the Lord. We can have business meetings, counseling appointments, coffee dates, play dates, strategic plans, budget conversations, and social gatherings all near and around a place where God rests.

A house of prayer with a regular rhythm provides an environment where people can regularly do life near and around the presence of the Lord. People regularly being in proximity to the presence of the Lord will transform communities. His presence can transform anyone and anything, and I believe this is God's desire for all people: a resting place for His presence.

Chapter 9

MARANATHA

Jesus is returning.

This reality will become more and more central to the church in the days ahead. The subject of the Lord's return has oftentimes been fogged over by charts, timelines, and predictions. I once heard an expert on the subject of Revelation say you should not teach from the book of Revelation unless you have studied it consistently for seven years. YIKES! That was not inspiring.

Maybe it hasn't totaled seven years, but after much personal study of the book of Revelation and the end time prophecies, I am convinced the heart of the matter is less about what will happen, and much more about why it will happen. While ample space and focus should be given to the what, in preparation for that hour, the why will provide sustaining grace for the end times.

Jesus Christ, whom God raised from the dead and who is currently seated at the right hand of His Father, is going to return soon. Only Jesus' Father knows the timing for His return, yet be assured, the Holy Spirit is preparing the earth for this moment.

MARANATHA

A peculiar word is found in the sixteenth chapter of First Corinthians. The entire New Testament is written in Ancient Greek, and Paul was addressing a predominantly Greek-speaking community when he wrote to the Corinthians in their native tongue. First Corinthians has 16 chapters; there are 437 verses and just under 10,000 words, and the book concludes with Paul using an Aramaic word—Maranatha.

This word is peculiar because the audience reading this letter was not the ancient, mostly Semitic, Middle Eastern Arameans. The likely readers were either Greek-speaking Jews, or Romans. Neither audience would have understood anything in Aramaic. So, it begs the question as to why Paul would throw in this particular word at the end of his first letter?

In a modern context, it would be like me writing this entire book in English and concluding this final chapter with a French slang word. You would either be familiar with the word contextually or somehow know what the word meant. Yet, if you did not know French, you would be in the dark about the meaning of the word. This would not make sense to you as the reader and possibly bring into question my ability to communicate as a leader or writer.

The meaning of the word maranatha is up for debate. Here's the question at hand: what tense is the word written in? In Aramaic, one could read it in either past, present, or future tense depending on how the syllables are arranged. *Vine's Complete Expository* Dictionary gives three potential definitions for the word maranatha: "The first part (Maran), ending in 'n,' signifies 'Lord'; as to the second part, the Fathers regarded it as a past tense, 'has come.' Modern expositors take it as equivalent to a present, 'cometh,' or future, 'will come.'"

The most common translation in the English Bible for maranatha is "Come Lord Jesus." This is the present tense reading. If translated in the past tense maranatha would mean, "Lord Jesus has come." Yet again, maranatha could also be read in a future tense "Our Lord is coming."

So, depending on how the letters are arranged in the original context, this one word could have one of three meanings:

- Come Lord Jesus
- Lord Jesus has come
- Our Lord is coming

So, what is the correct interpretation of this word? The answer is YES. All three.

The simplicity of the word's meaning, regardless of tense, is profound. In just one word, you have the gospel message: Jesus, come! Jesus came! Jesus is coming!

Maranatha.

Many scholars believe this phrase had become a secret "watch word" of sorts for the early and persecuted church. Most think it became a greeting among early believers to encourage them and identify those of the faith. Instead of shaking hands and saying "hello" or "what's up," they would say this one-word salutation: "Maranatha."

This would have been a word that neither the Greeks nor Romans understood. It infused hope into believers that were persecuted for their faith by their countrymen and most likely had to selectively and discreetly gather amongst themselves.

This early church maranatha message has, and still is becoming, very real to the UPPERROOM community. We are growing in awareness and understanding that the one who came is coming back.

A maranatha cry comes from a heart that is lovesick for the fulfillment of all that Jesus paid for. It is the cry from a bride who has been forever marked by His first coming, and longs for His second coming. The maranatha cry comes from those grateful for the Spirit of adoption that cries out "Abba, Father," but who also live in the tension of the Kingdom-now and the Kingdom-not-yet.

While we live in the mandate that He's called us to extend His Kingdom and destroy the works of the devil in His name, we also long for the day when He will make all wrong things right. He will wipe every tear from our eyes. He will establish justice on the earth.

Let's explore how the maranatha message points to the metanarrative of the gospel and the plan of redemption that God set in place before the foundation of the world.

HIS RETURN: THE FULFILLMENT OF THE GOSPEL

A growing revelation around the finished works of Jesus has emerged in the church over the last decade. I am so grateful for the emphasis on what Christ has accomplished for us at Calvary. The finished work of the cross is sufficient for anyone, anywhere, to enter into a relationship with God by faith in Jesus.

Yet, as we celebrate what transpired at Calvary, we need to also understand that the plan of redemption is not yet finished. The finished work of salvation (the cross) is unto the complete redemption of all that God has created, which will be fulfilled at the second coming of Jesus.

The theological terms are understood to be justification, sanctification, and glorification. This involves salvation in three tenses—past, present, and future—and also applies to the three parts of an individual—soul, spirit, and body.

The clearest way I have taught this threefold salvation is by looking at the word DONE. If you look closely, the word DONE actually has three words in it: DONE, DO, and ONE. These three words sum up the work of Calvary.

DONE

The first aspect of salvation is called justification. This is a finished and "DONE" reality. There is nothing one can do to become justified before God except to put their faith in the finished work of the cross. Justification is the term used to describe one's legal standing before God as a believer. Once born again, a believer's spirit is made new, alive, perfect, and one with God. This legal standing before God means that the individual has been made holy and blameless. The penalty of sin has been removed, resulting in all guilt, shame, and condemnation being removed through the perfect sacrifice of Jesus. This is a past tense reality that secures our position eternally before God.

DO

The second aspect of our salvation is called sanctification. Sanctification is the process of the "DONE" working its way into our souls. If the "DONE" (justification) applies to your spirit, the "DO" is applied to your soul (mind, will, and emotions). This is the process of growing and maturing into the grace of Jesus as His disciple. If the justified state of a believer is a seed in their heart, the sanctification process is the maturing of that seed in our soul. As our mind, will, and emotions are submitted to the grace of Jesus Christ, one grows in the reality of what Jesus has provided. This also applies to the power of sin in a believer's life—we are no longer slaves to sin (Rom. 6:1-7).

ONE

Glorification is the final work of salvation. The glorification of believers will happen at the second coming of Jesus. When He returns, we will be given new, resurrected, and glorified bodies. Upon this glorification, all of creation will be reconciled to God and set free from the corruption and power of sin. This will ultimately remove the very presence of any, and all, sin on the earth.

Hence, it is valid to say that salvation is a past, present, and future reality. You have been saved, you are being saved, and you will be saved. While your salvation is totally dependent on Jesus' work alone, it is applied in these three ways to the life, spirit, and soul of the believer.

The fulfillment of the gospel will not take place until Jesus returns.

Revelation 21:1-4 provides a description of how all that was lost because of sin will be restored in the new heaven and new earth. In Acts 3, after Peter proclaimed the gospel, he emphatically stated the necessity of repentance and returning to the Lord for the forgiveness of sins.

> So repent [change your inner self—your old way of thinking, regret past sins] and return [to God—seek His purpose for your life], so that your sins may be wiped away [blotted out, completely erased], so that times of refreshing may come

from the presence of the Lord [restoring you like a cool wind on a hot day]; and that He may send [to you] Jesus, the Christ, who has been appointed for you, whom heaven must keep until the time for the [complete] restoration of all things about which God promised through the mouth of His holy prophets from ancient time.

—Acts 3:19-21, AMP.

This is a threefold invitation from Peter:

1. Receive forgiveness of sins.

2. Present times of refreshing are coming in the presence of Jesus.

3. God is sending Jesus back to earth from heaven to restore all things.

This restoration of all things will complete God's plan of redemption for His entire created order. Literally, everything will be restored back to its original design.

The return of Jesus is the restoration of God's lost temple-city that we discussed in chapter two. The realities in Eden will again be restored. Revelation 21 describes this reality:

Then I saw a new heaven and a new earth; for the first heaven and the first earth had passed away (vanished), and there is no longer any sea. And I saw the holy city, new Jerusalem, coming down out of heaven from God, arrayed like a bride adorned for her husband; and then I heard a loud voice from the throne, saying, "See! The tabernacle of God is among men, and He will live among them, and they will be His people, and God Himself will be with them [as their God,] and He will wipe away every tear from their eyes; and there will no longer be death; there will no longer be sorrow and anguish, or crying, or pain; for the former order of things has passed away." And He who sits on the throne said, "Behold, I am making all things new." Also He said, "Write, for these words are faithful and true [they are accurate, incorruptible, and trustworthy]."

—Revelation 21:1-5

This is the restoration of all things. The effects, impact, and presence of sin will be removed completely. The garden reality that was lost will be regained. The one who came is coming back. The return of Jesus is less about charts, dates, and timelines. It is unto the eternal reality of a new heaven and new earth. While I am thankful for the growing emphasis on eschatology, we must understand the end times (and Jesus' return) is a crucial part of the gospel itself. The second coming of Jesus is not to be relegated as a peripheral subject, but rather central to our entire relationship with Jesus.

I believe the Holy Spirit is awakening the bride with a longing for His pending return. Revelation 22:17 says, "The Spirit and the bride say 'Come.'" This could actually translate that the Holy Spirit inside the bride says "Come." The idea of the Spirit and the bride make up a cumulative force beckoning the return of the Bridegroom. This cry will emerge across the globe in God's people joyfully and eagerly anticipating the return of Jesus.

The single word, maranatha, connects us to that coming reality.

In 2021, the Lord led our church community into forty days of prayer and fasting. We focused on what we called the "Maranatha Cry"—a cry for

God to prepare His bride for His return, and a prayer that we would live all our lives with an eternal perspective. On the first night of our fast, our young adult pastor, Aaron Smith (and a spiritual brother of mine), had a dream. In our community, we believe God still speaks and leads through dreams, and therefore we take dreams seriously. To illustrate the importance of a heavenly perspective, I would like to share Aaron's dream here.

In Aaron's words:

> The dream started and I saw Jesus standing in a palace. The palace looked like something from an old Prince of Egypt movie. It was late in the night, and Jesus was quietly walking through the palace to get to a room that I knew was special to Him. In the dream, I knew that Jesus and the palace were both in heaven. As Jesus was making His way to the room, I knew He was being stealthy about it because there were people who didn't think it was yet His time. But Jesus finally made His way to the room, and when He walked in, I saw that it was a large room with high ceilings and there were tall, large candles burning in the room. Maybe six or seven of these candles. In the center of the room was a large carpet. I watched Jesus walk to the center of the carpet and get on His knees. He bowed His head like He was going to pray, but instead of praying, He opened His ears and began hearing the prayers

THE SECOND COMING OF JESUS IS NOT TO BE RELEGATED AS A PERIPHERAL SUBJECT, BUT RATHER CENTRAL TO OUR ENTIRE RELATIONSHIP WITH JESUS.

of Christians on the earth. Instantly, my view zoomed into one of the prayers, and I saw the UPPERROOM full of people praying and fasting. I specifically remember everyone in the UPPERROOM praying for Jesus' return saying, "You can come, will you come?!" The dream zoomed back to heaven, and as Jesus was listening on His knees, suddenly guards filled the room (which I felt represented angels), and they all began to shout with one voice "YOU CAN GO!!" It sounded as if it was the voice of the Father coming through the guards. Jesus stood up, and as He did, Jesus and the entire palace were instantly in Jerusalem. Jesus had brought His entire palace to Israel. And then I woke up.

Aaron's dream, given by God at a critical juncture for our community, reminds me that there is a reality greater than what we see with our natural eyes. We were gathering daily to pray, and heaven was responding! Jesus was listening! He is bending His ear to our little prayers! We must lift our eyes, watch, and wait for Him to come. There is a metanarrative—a heavenly storyline that we are invited to participate in. The maranatha cry will result in a few key theological emphases. This list is not exhaustive by any means but can serve as an initial compass for you to engage the maranatha mandate.

EVANGELISM

The first emphasis will be on the harvest. While I have not spoken a lot about reaching people with the gospel in this book, the result of these eternal revelations, and the maranatha message, will be souls. Jesus said in Matthew 24:14, "This gospel of the Kingdom shall be preached in the whole world as a testimony to all the nations, and then the end will come." This is a profound reality for the end time generation.

The gospel will be preached in every nation, to every tongue, before the return of Jesus. Modern missiologists believe this will be accomplished in this decade (writing in 2022).

The only answer for the crisis surrounding the end time tribulations will be the gospel. I believe in the midst of wars, rumors of wars, and the surrounding shakings of the end times (as described in Matthew 24), the gospel message will thrive. It will truly be the greatest hour for a harvest of souls.

UNITY

Disunity is rampant today. Socially, politically, and spiritually, we are divided. The maranatha cry provides a simplicity for us as believers to unify and rally around. Many times, the church promotes unity initiatives for the sake of unity. Yet, we cannot unify around unity. As strange as that sounds, unity for unity's sake creates a shallowness to the church. We are not called to unify around unity—we are called to unify around the gospel. The maranatha message accomplishes this goal. This message transcends denominational, theological, and traditional obstacles that have divided the church in the past.

CLARITY

The maranatha message will bring needed clarity to people in the days ahead.

Andy Stanley says that uncertainty is not an indication of poor leadership; it underscores the need for leadership. It is the environment in which good leadership is most easily identified. Uncertainty is the reason we need leadership.

We must understand that uncertain times demand clarity. While we may not know everything, we must be clear in what we do know. There will be a number of cultural narratives that emerge in that hour that will attempt to answer the demand for solutions. Yet, the biblical narrative must be clear and accessible to all people. This is where the maranatha message will ring loud and clear.

Jesus warned His disciples not to be misled or deceived in the days that we are living in currently. You may wonder—how will deception come? It will come through the confusion that many will face because of the looming uncertainty around His return. Everything that can be shaken will be shaken (Heb. 12:27). This will be one of the most glorious yet challenging times in human history. The maranatha message will give believers "scriptural handles" to hold on to during these shakings. Without clarity around the biblical narrative of His return, people will fall into deception out of desperation and confusion.

ISRAEL

As the maranatha message increases, so will people's awareness of God's purpose and plan for Israel. This is central to the maranatha cry—the One who is returning will return to a specific place with a purpose and a plan.

As Zechariah prophesied (12:10), the Jews will mourn for and long for the One they pierced. In that hour, He will return to His land and His people to redeem them. We, as Gentiles, have been grafted into the plan of redemption that has not been fully fulfilled according to the Abrahamic covenant.

This is a massive topic that will not be undertaken in this chapter, but it must be mentioned. God desires to dwell in Jerusalem (Psalm 132:13-14). His resurrected feet will stand on the Mount of Olives and cross the Kidron Valley (Zech. 14:4). He will enter through the eastern gate of the Temple Mount and establish His Kingdom on the earth. This will be the glorious crescendo of the maranatha cry and will usher in the age to come.

We must see, understand, and grow in the knowledge of God's purposes for Israel in the days ahead. She is still the apple of His eye and the chosen people to bring forth His redemption. This was true and evident at His first coming and will be true and evident at His second coming. The maranatha message will help bring clarity and wisdom to these purposes.

THE PRESENCE OF GOD

In the days ahead, the Holy Spirit will prepare the earth for the return of Jesus. Upon His arrival, a prepared, mature, and ready bride will await Him. Ephesians 5:27 gives evidence that He is preparing her by His word to be presented gloriously. She will have no spot, wrinkle, or blemish, but will be holy and blameless. This will be His work in His people.

Therefore, it could be said that the Holy Spirit will function in the days ahead as a wedding planner. The Father has sent the Spirit to prepare a worthy bride for His Son. This is no small event.

Every nation, every language, every human being throughout history will be judged and either included or excluded from this ceremony. There will be no neutral ground in that moment. Those readied will join the marriage supper and those who are not will be excluded and removed. Make no mistake about it, this is what the maranatha cry is unto—a wedding.

This is why His House will be marked by His Presence in the last days of human history. A glorious outpouring of the Holy Spirit will prepare mankind for the appointed date. The Father of glory is sending the Holy Spirit to the earth with this date in mind.

The maranatha cry is the most strategic and simple way to communicate this coming reality. The God who came is coming back. The maranatha message will fuel evangelism, the great commission, endurance in trial, and perspective—it is the "blessed hope" of the church. We must tether our hearts to this reality in order to sustain our faith in the days ahead.

When the Son of Man returns, He will look for faith on the earth (Luke 18:8). This faith will exist in one of the most tumultuous hours the earth has ever known. Injustice will be rampant. Deception will be rampant. Persecution will come to those who stand in His truth and under His word. Yet, the maranatha cry is the anthem for the end times church awaiting His return.

CONCLUDING THOUGHTS

It is February of 2023 as I finish writing this book. There are revival reports beginning to emerge from a few college campuses around the United States. What started at a normal chapel service at Asbury University is currently a multi-week prayer and worship service. It is not marked by preaching (although that has happened) and it is not marked by evangelism (although people are getting saved), but it is marked by the manifestation of God's presence. His nearness being experienced, and lives being transformed by it.

"God is here" is the consistent description of what is taking place at Asbury and subsequent universities. The reason they continue to worship is because they don't want to stop.

Moreso, reports are growing of churches that are hosting non-stop prayer and worship gatherings. "Burn the playbook" wrote one pastor, as he and his church entered their 38th hour of worship and prayer (after their Sunday morning service time would have normally concluded).

This is beautiful and needed. Cultural Christianity is not going to cut it in the days ahead. God is preparing us by building "arks" that will sustain the outpouring that is coming. Day and night prayer will be normative in every city across the globe.

It won't be marked by style or expression, but by the presence of God. It won't be about frequency or intensity, but about the consistent outpouring of God's presence into communities that won't change the subject. They will honor, respond, and learn how to continually host Him.

I am expectant that this will become normative in the church at large. There will be varying distinctions and avenues to this end, but the end will be Him. His dwelling in our midst in greater ways—an undeniable manifestation of God's presence on earth.

The Gospel is unto this end. I realize that by faith we have Him fully, yet our experience of this will grow in greater measures globally as His second coming nears.

My prayer is that this book has put a framework for what this could look like in the coming days. I am also convinced that there are very practical ways to establish and sustain these environments. This work was to frame the UPPERROOM story and culture, and is foundational to the numerous resources, materials and teachings we offer at UPPERROOM (upperroom.co). The practical values and practices that have ensued since our first prayer meeting in 2010 are another conversation I hope to have with you in the days ahead, as we all wait, prepare and long for His blessed return.

Maranatha.

Miller

APPENDIX & RESOURCES

Beale, Gregory K. "Eden, The Temple, and the Church's Mission in the New Creation." Journal of the Evangelical Theological Society, March 1, 2005. https://www.etsjets.org/files/JETS-PDFs/48/48-1/48-1-pp005-031_JETS.pdf

Middleton, J. R. The Liberating Image: The Imago Dei in Genesis 1 (Grand Rapids: Brazos, 2005), 81; cf. R. P. Gordon, "The Week That Made the World: Reflections on the First Pages of the Bible," in Reading the Law: Studies in Honour of Gordon J. Wenham, ed. J. G. McConville and Karl Möller, LHBOTS 461 (Edinburgh: T&T Clark, 2007), 234–37.

Walton, J.H. "Creation in Genesis 1:1–2:3 and the Ancient Near East." Calvin Theological Journal, 48–63. 2008. https://wisdomintorah.com/wp-content/uploads/Creation-in-Gen-1-1-to-2-3-and-the-ANE-Order-out-of-DIsorder-after-Chaoskampf-Walton.pdf

Walton, J.H. "Creation," in Dictionary of the Old Testament: Pentateuch, ed. T. D. Alexander and D. W. Baker (Downers Grove, IL:

InterVarsity, 2003), 161. Cf. J. H. Walton, The Lost World of Genesis One: Ancient Cosmology and the Origins Debate (Downers Grove, IL: IVP Academic, 2009), 72–86.

G. J. Wenham, "Sanctuary Symbolism in the Garden of Eden Story," PW-CJS 9 (1986): 19.

Wiersbe, Warren W. Wiersbe's Expository Outlines on the New Testament. Wheaton, Ill.: Victor Books. 1992.

SEVEN OLD TESTAMENT "REVIVALS" THAT INCORPORATED DAVIDIC WORSHIP

David's Worship Reformation: he established 4,000 musicians, 288 singers (12 x 24 = 288) and 4,000 gatekeepers. Consequently, financed about 10,000 people on his "full-time staff" to facilitate worship and offerings to God. 1 Chronicles 25:7 "So the number of them, with their brethren who were instructed in the songs of the Lord, all who were skillful, was two hundred and eighty-eight." 1 Chronicles 23:5 ...four thousand were gatekeepers, and four thousand praised the Lord with musical instruments, "which I made," said David, "for giving praise."

Jehoshaphat's reform (about 870 BC) included establishing singers and musicians. 19 "The Levites...stood up to praise the Lord..." 21" He appointed those who should sing to the Lord..." 28 "They came...with stringed instruments...to the house of the Lord" (2 Chr. 20:19-28).

Jehoiada the priest, two kings after Jehoshaphat, restored temple worship in the order of David (about 835 B.C) with singers, etc. Jehoiada appointed the oversight of the house of the Lord to...the Levites... to offer the burnt offerings...with rejoicing and with singing, as it was established by David (2 Chr. 23:18).

Hezekiah's revival (about 725 BC) included restoring singers/musicians as David commanded. 25 "He stationed the Levites in the house of the Lord with...stringed instruments...according to the commandment of David..." 27 "The song of the LORD began..." (2 Chr. 29:25-27).

Josiah's revival (about 625 BC) restored full-time singers and musicians as David commanded. 3 He said to the Levites...4 "Prepare yourselves...following the instruction of David..." 15 "The singers...were in their places, according to the command of David..." (2 Chr. 35:3-15).

Zerubbabel (about 536 BC) established full-time singers and musicians as commanded by David. 10 "The Levites...to praise the LORD, according to the ordinance of David" (Ezra 3:10-11).

Ezra and Nehemiah (445 BC) established full-time singers and musicians as David commanded. 24 "The Levites...give thanks...according to the command of David..." 45 "The singers and the gatekeepers kept the charge of God...according to the command of David..." (Neh. 12:24, 45).

AUTHOR ACKNOWLEDGEMENTS

Lorisa, my bride and best friend. We debated whether we should co-author this book because so much of the story and revelation is our collective journey. Instead, you edited, rewrote, crafted and shaped this book—as you have this entire journey. You are the love of my life. You also are the purest, wholehearted, devoted lover of Jesus that I have ever known. You are the smartest person in the room and the lowliest. You are the MVP of our family. I absolutely adore everything about you.

My parents, George and Carolyn Miller. My love for the local church came from my upbringing. This book is the fruit of your faith. Albeit the fruit took time and maybe looks different than you would have thought—make no mistake that this is your fruit, Mom and Dad. Thank you for loving Jesus and building His church over the last 70+ years. I love you and honor you.

UPPERROOM Elders—the best shepherds I have ever had the privilege to serve under. Your love for Jesus, His Word and His people is unprecedented for me. This book is the fruit of your leadership and trust.

Autumn Williams, what role have you not played at UPPERROOM? Music, pastoring, events, planting, and now publisher/editor. You are wonder woman. Thank you for tirelessly serving the vision of this book and all the people it represents. You are a treasure to everyone you know, a dear friend of ours, and an even dearer friend to Jesus. You give and give and give more. I am indebted and grateful.

Sarah Jimenez, you make my professional world turn. Thank you for your grace, patience and consistency. You and Jony have been integral in all things UPPERROOM. I am so very grateful for the way you have served Lo and I over the years.